D1481047

STATE OF EMERGENCY
WE <u>MUST</u> SAVE
AFRICAN AMERICAN
MALES

JAWANZA KUNJUFU

Chicago, Illinois

Front Cover illustration by Tony Quaid
Copyright © 2001 by Jawanza Kunjufu
First Edition, First Printing

Printed in the United States of America

ISBN: 0-913543-73-X

CONTENTS

PREFACE

I have prayed for the Holy Spirit to exude through me His wisdom, excellence, and accuracy and for the anointing to be throughout the writing of this entire book. I also pray that you, the reader, will hear what the Holy Spirit would say to you.

There are demons, principalities, and rulers in high places destroying African American males. The Bible reminds us that the weapons of our warfare are not carnal but mighty in God for the pulling down of strongholds. We struggle not against flesh and blood but against principalities and rulers in high places. We must bind those demons, principalities, and rulers in high places. It's the believer's job to break the strongholds.

This problem has been with us for a very long time. When I wrote Volume I of my bestseller, *Countering the Conspiracy to Destroy Black Boys* in 1982, there were less than 100,000 African American males in jail. Today, there are in excess of 1.3 million African American males involved in the penal system. [1] The demons, principalities, rulers, and strongholds have become stronger, and it will take more than our human effort in order to save our males. The incarceration of African American males in the last two decades has had a more detrimental effect on the Black family than 246 years of slavery. What happens to a community that loses one-third of its men? Who will protect elders, women, and children from bullies? Who will resist blatant acts of police brutality? The few remaining men in Cincinnati rose up and said in the spirit of Fannie Lou Hamer, "I'm sick and tired of being sick and tired." We must invite the Holy Spirit into this movement, and yield to His leading into order to save African American males.

DEDICATION

This book is dedicated to the *1,200 African American men of the 364th infantry, U.S. Army*. In 1943, during the height of the Jim Crow era; these men were slaughtered in Centreville, Mississippi, by U.S. military police. Originally they were members of a regiment of 3,000 African American soldiers stationed in Arizona. The U.S. military did not like their spirit, so they broke them up. Eighteen hundred men were shipped to one part of the country, and the 1,200 men, identified as leaders, were sent to Mississippi and killed, their bodies dumped in a salt mine. Parents were told that their sons had died in action. This might have been yet another sad event omitted from the history books had it not been for Carrol Cose, a White author, who learned about the atrocity from a surviving military police officer. She spent the next 13 years doing research and finally documented her findings in a book titled *The Slaughter*.

To *Johnny Gammage*. In 1996, Gammage was pulled over by police while driving his cousin's Jaguar in suburban Pittsburgh at 2:00 a.m. Five Brentwood police officers arrived on the scene. One officer said that Gammage ran three red lights *after* he flashed his lights. The officer ordered Gammage out of the car and saw him grab something that he claimed was a weapon, but in reality was only a cellular phone. The officer knocked the phone out of Gammage's hand and a scuffle followed. One officer put a foot on Gammage's neck while another beat him with a flashlight, baton, and a blackjack. Gammage died handcuffed, ankles bound, faced down on the pavement, unarmed.

To *Amadou Diallo*. On February 4, 1999, four White police officers gunned down Diallo as he entered the vestibule of his Bronx home. They fired 41 shots from nine-millimeter pistols, hitting Diallo 19 times. The officers said that a wallet in the young man's hand looked like a gun. The officers were acquitted of all charges.

To *Abner Louima*. On August 13, 1997, Louima was arrested and taken to the Brooklyn police department. Four officers were accused of inserting the handle of a toilet plunger into his rectum, which caused severe damage to his small intestine and gall bladder.

To *James Byrd*. On June 7, 1998, Byrd was walking home in Jasper County Texas, when three intoxicated White males spray painted him, pulled his pants down, cut his throat, and chained his ankles to their pickup truck. They dragged his body three miles, literally destroying his body and decapitating his head.

To *Jeronimo Pratt*. In 1968, Pratt was accused of murdering a teacher in Santa Monica. He was convicted and served 27 years in jail for a crime he did not commit. A former FBI agent confirmed that Pratt had been framed and was actually in Oakland at the time of the murder.

To *Fred Finley*. On June 22, 2000, Finley was killed by security officers at the Lord & Taylor in Dearborn, Michigan. While Finley was shopping, his daughter stole a $4 bracelet. Although he spent $200 on items purchased at the store, he was accosted by security because of the stolen bracelet. They placed a chokehold on Fred Finley, and he died shortly afterward.

To *James Dawson*. On November 5, 1999, the 37 year-old parking lot attendant was detained at the Cumberland County correctional facility, 225 miles south of Chicago, for speeding. The police arrested him because his license was suspended. He was taken to jail and bail was set at $150. His mother, brother, and a grandson arrived at the facility the next day to post bail and were told to wait outside for Dawson. He was never released. An ambulance pulled up to the jail and took James Dawson to the hospital, where he was pronounced dead on arrival. The mother was denied the opportunity to view the body. Officials claimed Dawson had committed suicide, but the body was returned to the funeral home without blood and missing several body parts and organs. Dawson was not an organ donor[2].

To the hundreds of innocent citizens in Los Angeles who were victims of police corruption. Officer Rafael Perez, a member of CRASH (Community Resources Against Street Hoodlums), told police officials, only after being caught stealing eight pounds of cocaine worth $1 million that he and his colleagues stole drugs, murdered innocent people, and falsified evidence. Twenty police officers have been fired, 30 have been convicted, and 70 more are under investigation. Hundreds of African Americans and Latinos who were convicted, are now being released.[3]

To *Charles and Etta Carter.* This elderly African American couple from Pennsylvania who were stopped in 1997 by Maryland State Police on their 40th wedding anniversary. Troopers searched their car and brought in drug sniffing dogs. During the course of the search, their daughter's wedding dress was tossed out of the car and onto the ground. Mrs. Carter was not allowed to use the restroom during the search because police officers feared she would flee. Their belongings were strewn along the highway, trampled, and urinated on by the dogs. No drugs were found and no ticket was issued.

To *Nelson Walker.* In 1998, the North Carolina college student was driving along I-95 in Maryland when he was pulled over by state police. They accused him of not wearing a seat belt. The officers detained him and his two passengers for two hours as they searched for illegal drugs, weapons, and other contraband. After finding nothing in the car, they proceeded to dismantle the car, removing part of the door panel, a seat panel, and part of the sunroof. When they finished, an officer handed Walker a screwdriver and said, "You're going to need this."

To *Danny Glover*, who makes millions of dollars as a star and producer of films, but unfortunately, like any other African American male, has difficulty securing a taxi. To *Alonzo Jackson.* One day Jackson went to an Eddie Bauer clothing store in Temple Hills, Maryland, to shop. He just happened to be wearing a shirt previously purchased from the store. Jackson was accused of stealing the shirt and was told to produce a receipt. He didn't have a receipt, so he was detained and accused of theft. Later, he returned to the store with the receipt and a promise that his family would sue the Eddie Bauer Company.

To *all African American males in Cincinnati* who, tired of being murdered by the police, rose up and shut the city down.

Finally, to *Lionel Tate*, one of 10,000 African American juveniles serving time in adult facilities. On July 28, 1999, Tate killed a six-year-old girl in Florida. The defense attorney's position was that as he was helping his mother baby-sit the girl and that Tate demonstrated some techniques he had observed on a Wrestling Federation television program. Unfortunately, the jury did not see it that way, and on January 16, 2001, Tate was convicted and sentenced to life without parole.

INTRODUCTION

At what point does the madness stop? There was a time when one of every ten African American males was involved in the penal system. Later it became one of five then one of four, and now it is one of three. It is projected that by 2020, two of every three African American males will be involved in the penal system![4] The madness must stop. We must declare a state of emergency. The African American community cannot go on like this.

How can a community, how can a people, how can families survive if 68 percent of the children do not have a father in the home? We must declare a state of emergency and we must marshal all of our resources, not only in Black America, but also in White America. More than three decades ago, Malcolm X wanted to take our case before the United Nations. We must reconsider this strategy because our community cannot continue in the direction that it's heading.

This book is divided into eight chapters. The first chapter provides a quantitative analysis of the state of emergency by comparing White America with Black America. If Whites had our problems, they would not allow them to continue.

Chapter two is about the miseducation of our children. In kindergarten, the number of boys equals the number of girls; by eighth grade, twelfth grade, and college, girls far outnumber boys. What can we learn from the educational system? Is there a relationship between special education and prison? Is there a relationship between Ritalin and cocaine? Is illiteracy a precursor for incarceration? Is zero tolerance the best way to intervene when youth get into trouble? Could you have lived your life under a zero tolerance regime?

The American economic system is explored in chapter three. We live in a country that is patriarchal and capitalistic. Is it possible for a male without capital (money) to be a man in a capitalistic country? Can a male be a man without employment? Why were Africans brought to this country? Does that reason exist today? Does America have a problem? What do they do with people they no longer need?

In the fourth chapter, the drug industry is examined. Is there really a war on drugs, or is it a war on African people and people of color? America may be losing the war on drugs, but winning the war on African American males. What can we learn from other countries? Why does America, with only six percent of the world's population, consume more than 60 percent of all drugs? What can we learn from China, Japan, and European countries?

Chapter five deals with the penal system. An entire book could have been written about prisons. America leads the world in incarceration rates, homicides, and drug consumption. Why? If we're trying to balance the budget, why are we sending more males to jail for longer periods of time? If the goal of prison is rehabilitation as well as punishment, then why are recidivism rates between 60 and 80 percent? Why are we privatizing prisons? Does privatization result in lower recidivism rates? Does America believe incarceration will solve its problems? Is America willing to allocate one-third of its budget to the penal system?

What has been the effect of the penal system on the African American family? That question is answered in chapter six. Fatherlessness is a disease that affects the entire country, but it has reached epidemic proportions in the African American community. Visit a classroom in any low-income area and ask the children to raise their hands if they have a father in the home—very few hands will be raised. What are the affects of fatherlessness on children's self-esteem, academic performance, sexuality, propensity of becoming incarcerated, and drug use? These questions and others are addressed in this chapter.

We'll also look at the impact the state of emergency has placed on African American mothers, most of whom are raising children alone. Throughout the entire book, and especially in chapter seven, solutions will be offered.

The problems facing Black America reflect a deeper problem in White America. If 52 percent of White men reported they were victims of racial profiling, White America would call that a state of emergency. America is on a collision course with Rome, Sodom, and Gomorrah, Santee, Columbine, Peducah, Pearl, Fayetteville, Jonesboro, Edinboro, and Springfield; these are not anomalies.

This is not a Black problem, nor is it an education, economic, prison, or drug problem. This is a moral problem which requires moral solutions.

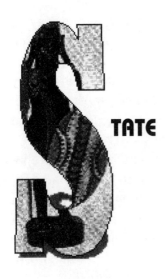**TATE**

OF

**MERGENCY**

1

If one of every three White males were involved in the penal system, White America would declare a **state of emergency.**

If 80 percent of the White children in
special education classes were male,
White America would declare a
state of emergency.

If there were three White females
for every one White male on college
campuses, White America
would declare a
state of emergency.

If White women had the life
expectancy of African American
males—65 years—White America
would declare a
state of emergency.
(By the way, White women have a
life expectancy of 79 years.)

If one of every 12 White males in Washington, D.C., were a victim of homicide, White America would declare a **state of emergency.**

If 31 percent of White males in Alabama and Florida were permanently disenfranchised, White America would declare a **state of emergency.**

If 14 percent of White males nationwide were temporarily disenfranchised,
White America would declare a
state of emergency.

If AIDS was the number one killer
of White males, White America
would declare a
state of emergency.

If Whites were 13 percent
of the population, but comprised
35 percent of drug arrests,
55 percent of drug convictions,
and 74 percent of drug prisoners,
White America would declare a
state of emergency.

If Whites comprised 17 percent
of drivers on the Maryland state
highway, but 70 percent of drivers
stopped by the police,
White America would declare a
state of emergency.

If prosecutors sought the death penalty 70 percent of the time when a White person killed an African American, but only 19 percent of the time when it was reversed, White America would declare a **state of emergency.**

If 40 percent of White males were illiterate in America, White America would declare a **state of emergency.**

If Whites were 13 percent
of the population, but 50 percent
of those waiting on death row,
White America would declare a
state of emergency.

If Whites were 13 percent of the population, but 67 percent of the juveniles in adult courts and 77 percent of the juveniles in adult prisons, White America would declare a **state of emergency.**

If only one of every 13 White babies were born out of wedlock in 1965, but seven of every ten in 2001, White America would call this a **state of emergency.**

If the life expectancy of White males
in Washington, D.C. was only 57
years, and there was no state
with a White male life expectancy
greater than 70 years,
White America would call it a
state of emergency.

If Whites represented 84 percent of crack cocaine convictions, White America would declare a **state of emergency.**

If two of every three White males
were projected to be involved
in the penal system by 2020,
White America would call it a
state of emergency.

All this is true in Black America, [5]
so when are we going to rise up
and declare
state of emergency?

TATE

OF

MERGENCY

2

THE MISEDUCATION OF
AFRICAN AMERICAN MALES

Once upon a time there was an experienced elementary school teacher who was having a very challenging year. A disproportionate number of African American males had been assigned to her class. Not only were they under performing, they were getting in constant trouble. She couldn't figure out how to help them improve their academic performance and reduce their disciplinary problems.

One day the principal was out of his office, so she sneaked a peak at the files of her problem male students. She wanted to understand the problem. In many of the folders she noticed numerical scores, including 109, 111, 113, 121, 126, etc. She was flabbergasted. No wonder classroom performance was so dismal. She hadn't been challenging her students enough! She had lowered her expectations and now saw the error of her ways.

She went back to her class, inspired with this new-found information, and proceeded to raise her expectations. She felt a greater bond with her students because she now realized their brilliance. She smiled and encouraged them more. She nurtured them and gave them words of encouragement. She brought in many outside resource materials for stimulation.

At the end of the school year, the children's scores were well above the national average. She was acknowledged throughout the city for her tremendous performance. Unable to keep her secret from the principal any longer, she confessed that she'd gone into his office and reviewed the children's files. The principal accepted her apology and then told her that those numbers were not IQ scores but locker room numbers!

For some that would be a fantastic story. To me it's a horror story. I wonder how many teachers are playing God with our children? How many teachers realize that they function as potters and children are their clay? They can shape them and mold them to be whatever they want. What would have happened if the teacher in the story hadn't gone into the principal's office? Suppose she had known the numbers were locker room numbers. The class would have continued to under perform and disciplinary problems would have persisted.

How many classes in America are under performing? How many boys have we lost because of teachers with low expectations and poor classroom management skills? How many doctors, dentists, engineers, and computer programmers have we lost? How many Ben Carsons, Keith Blacks, Johnny Cochrans, and Willie Garys have we lost in the miseducation system?

I receive hundreds of letters from concerned parents about their sons' school challenges. As a result, I have been forced to expand beyond my Chicago office to telephone counseling. The following letter is an example of the school problems parents are facing today. (Names have been deleted to protect their privacy.)

The Miseducation of African American Males

March 5, 2001

We are *deeply concerned* for the well being of our son, and his ability to learn in the environment and tone that you, and other staff have set for him in your school. It is our belief that the way that you are treating our son is deplorable and we can assure you that we will take every necessary step to protect his interests. Let us express that we are not hostile, nor should this letter be taken in that context—we feel that we must state that point of fact because we do not want to have that assumption made and have it somehow further shadow our son indirectly.

First, let me state that although the school is a Magnet School, we believe that *all* of your staff needs intensive diversity training, especially in the area of elementary education and the learning styles of minority children, particularly Black boys. It seems to me that the first course of action for little Black boys is always to place them in special education. This approach keeps them out of sight and out of mind from the mainstream learning environment. It is our belief (and that of many others who study this kind of activity in the education system of the United States) that this is the first step in conditioning little Black boys to believe that they are *inferior* and that they can only achieve on an inferior level.

Second, if, as you stated at your Instructional Support Team meeting, our son has displayed these "aggressive behaviors" from kindergarten to now, why was there no intervention prior to this? Why was it allowed to escalate to this level? Perhaps we could have avoided your current recommendation of special education placement for our son.

It is a fact that for as many teaching styles that exist, there are an equal, and perhaps greater number of learning styles for children. Our son is an *exceptionally bright* student who has the ability to do his grade level work and beyond. He has told us that he is frequently bored in his classroom. *That does not justify the unacceptable behaviors of which our son is always being accused, but we believe that it partially explains why he does not produce the expected output in the classroom.* He is a very animated, lively child and he enjoys learning new things. He becomes bored easily when not challenged, so perhaps your educators and administration need to consider that he is not challenged enough.

At home, he is encouraged to believe that he can achieve anything to which he sets his mind on achieving. We allow him to express himself creatively. We also set parameters for behavior, with rewards and consequences. We will *continue* to work with our son to ensure his success in completion of this and future school years.

I serve as a consultant to numerous school districts throughout the country. When I evaluate a school, I use the performance of African American males as the base. I compare the performance of African American males to African American females, White males, and especially White females. The American educational system upholds White females as the "ideal" students academically and socially; therefore, I use their performance as the benchmark. White America would declare a state of emergency if White females suffered the dismal educational status of African American males.

If a school is racially integrated (for example, 50 percent African American and 50 percent White; 25 percent each African American male, African American female, White male and White female), I'll ask the district superintendent and school principals the following questions:

If African American males are 25 percent of the student body, do they make up 25 percent of gifted and talented students? Honors classes and honor role students? Advanced placement classes? Remedial reading students? Special education students? Suspensions? Dropouts? Expulsions? How many African American males have been counseled for college admissions?

The obvious implication for African American females is that there will not be an adequate number of African American males down the pipeline as they both matriculate through elementary school, high school, and college, and into the workforce. Much will be said about this implication in the chapters on economics and fatherlessness.

In my book, *Adam, Where Are You? Why Most Black Men Don't Go to Church*, I asked my readers if they knew of just one Black church that has more African American males than females attending church on Sundays. There are about five churches in America that have more African American males than females. Likewise, I ask school administrators and educators nationwide if they know of any schools in which African American males are outperforming White females. If the school district is highly segregated, I ask if there are any schools in which African American males are outperforming African American females. Sadly, the answer is always the same: none.

In a study conducted in Milwaukee Wisconsin, the findings were alarming and, unfortunately, reflective of public schools throughout the nation. Of the approximately 5,700 African American males in high school, only two percent had a grade point average (GPA) greater than 3.0. In fact, 80 percent of all African American males in Milwaukee public schools had a GPA below 2.0. [6]

This is clearly a state of emergency. Milwaukee is not an anomaly. Most school districts unfortunately have a disproportionate percentage of African American males with GPAs below 2.0 and a very small percentage of African American males above 3.0.

I believe the three critical grades for African American males are kindergarten, fourth grade, and ninth grade.

Kindergarten

In 1995, the National Association for the Education of Young Children stated in its position paper that since kindergarten is a child's first opportunity for formal learning, kindergarten teachers must accept the different learning needs and social backgrounds of children. From the first day of class, young children who were raised in "at risk" environments are labeled "behind"; yet, how can a child be considered behind on the *first day* of kindergarten?

Why should kindergarten teachers divide children by ability as early as the first week of kindergarten? While there are no gifted, honors, or advanced placement kindergarten classes, many teachers divide students into fast and slow learning groups—e.g., reading groups called the eagles ("advanced"), robins ("intermediate"), and bluebirds ("slow"). The game of tracking and playing God begins early in many American schools. My concern is that a disproportionate percentage of African American males are being placed in the lowest reading and math groups. Teacher expectations are low and, as a result, many boys are failing kindergarten.

If you want to see God's awesome power, look at our boys in kindergarten. They are eager, curious, and full of questions. Schools often invite me to speak to and motivate older students, but I often wonder what was done in the early years to destroy their innocence, enthusiasm, curiosity, and motivation. Unfortunately, as students become older, they ask fewer questions. I believe the problem is systemic and not genetic. Whatever achievement gap exists among males and females, African Americans and Whites in kindergarten, it is much smaller than the gap that exists in eighth grade. School policies and practices widen the gap.

I am often been asked by school districts to "fix" students. The reality is that the system needs to be fixed. We must save our boys from being destroyed in kindergarten. Many teachers are aware that boys and girls mature at different levels. Research shows that boys' brains grow more slowly and do not catch up to girls until age 17. Boys generally learn to control their arms and legs before their fingers. In girls this is reversed. Girls in kindergarten can often draw tiny figures and pictures, yet may be seven or eight before they are able to run, jump, and catch a ball. Boys can often run and jump beautifully, long before they can hold a pencil or scissors. Only by age seven or eight do boys' nervous systems develop enough to enable them to sit still and hold their body erect while writing at a desk. [7]

How unfortunate it is that while teachers theoretically understand that boys and girls mature at different rates, they do not allow for those differences in the classroom. If boys have more advanced gross motor than fine motor skills, shouldn't teachers provide more objects in their lesson plans? To address the differences in boys' and girls' attention spans, why don't teachers alter their lesson plans to meet the number of minutes boys can spend on any one task? We know that boys have a higher energy level than girls, so why don't teachers allow more movement and activity in the classroom? Throughout this chapter and in the last chapter on solutions we will be providing strategies to address some of the challenges facing African American males in this state of emergency.

School districts must *mandate* that teachers take in-service training on Black male learning styles. It disappoints me greatly when I have to present a workshop at a school or school district where attendance is voluntary. The following are five types of educators who would benefit most from this type of in-service training:

1.   Referral agents. These teachers don't teach. They refer. Research shows that 20 percent of teachers make almost 80 percent of the referrals into special education and suspension. Referral agents seldom attend a voluntary workshop.

2.   Custodians. These teachers have been with a school district for many years—and they use the same lesson plans year after year. Their person code is, "If you don't bother me, I won't bother you." Unfortunately, custodians seldom attend a voluntary workshop.

3.   Instructors. These teachers believe they teach subjects and not children. They are math teachers, science teachers, and English teachers—and they mean that, literally. Unfortunately, from the fourth grade on up, there seems to be increasing numbers of instructors. Instructors seldom attend a voluntary workshop.

4.   Teachers. While teachers understand subject matter, they feel there should be congruence between pedagogy and learning styles. They believe that best practices is not about teaching the way you want to teach or the way it's always been done but the way children learn. If a classroom has mostly right brain thinkers, these teachers will adapt their methods and lesson plans to this style of learning. Teachers often attend voluntary workshops.

The following retention chart reflects how teachers disseminate information.

Average Retention Rate After 24 Hours

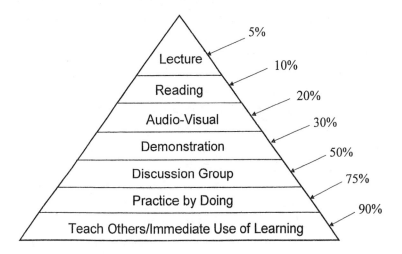

5.   Coaches. These teachers are experts at bringing together subject matter, pedagogy, and learning styles, but they also believe in bonding with, motivating, and enhancing the self-esteem of students. Coaches often attend voluntary workshops.

Referral agents, custodians, and instructors are the teachers most in need of attending in-service training on the learning styles and needs of Black males. Training will continue to be voluntary as long as referral agents, custodians, and instructors are promoted into administrative positions (e.g., principals, superintendents). Unfortunately, many African American school districts, schools, and classrooms are administrated and taught by referral agents, custodians, and instructors.

State of Emergency
We _Must_ Save African American Males

Few education departments in colleges and universities offer classes on Black male learning styles. My ultimate desire would be to keep African American boys in heterogeneous classrooms, but only with teachers and coaches. If schools are not willing to do that then my second recommendation would be to provide African American male classrooms.

There are approximately 500 African American male classrooms nationwide. Rather than accepting the disparity in performance between male and female students, creative principals have chosen to separate boys from girls. This has also been beneficial for females. Nationwide, there has been tremendous success with the implementation of Black male classrooms. I will say more about this strategy in the final chapter of this book.

Another strategy to help Black males would be to delay their entrance into kindergarten until they are six or seven years old. Children in Germany, Belgium, Switzerland, and many other European countries do not begin school until age seven. [8] (If strategies seem to work well in other countries, we should consider using them in America, especially if the educational experiences and performance of Black males can be maximized.)

These countries suffer no gender achievement gap. This is in contrast to America and many English-speaking countries where male students populate 80 percent of remedial reading classes. This is a very controversial recommendation, but if we know that boys and girls mature at different levels, why are we expecting boys to do what girls can do as early as five years of age?

Age is just one issue dealing with the bigger question of "school readiness." I would rather delay a child's entrance to kindergarten than set him up to fail. It is naive to think that all children of all races of both genders are on the same level at the magical age of five. It is also unfortunate that teachers expect all children of all races of both genders to be able to perform equally. It is also unfortunate that with an increasing number of mothers having to work outside the home and the declining percentage of fathers in the home, many mothers rely on public schools as early as five years of age to educate their children. The delaying of children into schools would cause problems for many parents.

Fourth Grade

The next critical grade for African American males is fourth grade. In my bestseller, *Countering the Conspiracy to Destroy Black Boys*, I wrote extensively about the fourth grade syndrome.[9] The following chart shows the gravity of the problem.

Beginning Third Grade Percentile	Ending Seventh Grade Percentile	Reading Progress (Years)
98	35	1.3
97	54	2.7
92	24	2.1
91	68	3.1
81	72	3.9
72	72	3.6
66	59	3.9
63	7	0.7
63	4	0.0
57	39	3.2
47	9	2.1
41	11	2.5
29	12	3.0
21	44	5.6
21	29	4.7
21	17	3.8
18	1	1.3
16	39	4.6
7	30	4.5
5	5	3.2

The following are some of the many causes of the fourth grade syndrome:

* As children grow older, teacher expectations and nurturing decrease.
* As children grow older, parent involvement decreases.
* Lesson plans for the early grades are right brain oriented; higher grades are more left-brain oriented.
* Peer pressure intensifies, as children get older.
* As children grow older, the amount of homework they receive from teachers, increases.

The following chart shows how boys respond to homework in comparison to girls. [10]

Percentage of Time Spent on Homework in 1996, by Sex

	Grade 4		Grade 8		Grade 12	
	Males	Females	Males	Females	Males	Females
Don't have	11.8	10.2	7.2	6.0	15.7	11.9
Don't do	4.4	1.6	9.6	4.9	13.2	3.1
½ hour or less	40.0	40.7	28.0	19.7	25.2	19.5
1 hour	27.7	30.9	34.0	38.7	25.4	30.0
1 hour or more	16.1	16.6	21.1	30.8	20.5	35.5
Total	100	100	100	100	100	100

Many boys have never experienced a male teacher. Some boys in fourth grade never have seen a Black man read a book, write a letter, operate a computer, or give any indication the he values academics. Many boys begin to get the impression that academics are for females and physical activities are for males.

The number of African American male teachers and teaching assistants must be increased. I've had many accomplishments of which I am most proud, but I must admit that

The Miseducation of African American Males

I am so grateful to God for using me to inspire hundreds of African American males to become elementary teachers, and I pray that as a result of this book and other avenues, that number will significantly increase.

Also, in this state of educational emergency, every African American male must volunteer in a school at least one day a month. Professional African American males should consider taking a one-year leave of absence from their jobs to teach in a public school, preferably at the fourth grade level.

I also recommend the development of a fourth grade intervention team. How is it that the government can find $18,000 to $38,000 to incarcerate a Black man but not a cent for fourth graders? The fourth grade intervention team would consist of educators, counselors, social workers, psychologists, ministers, entrepreneurs, community activists, and recreation specialists. These individuals would create a village around any male student at risk of significant academic decline. An ounce of prevention is far better than a pound of medicine.

Ninth Grade

The last critical grade is ninth grade. Many people think that when boys drop out of school they leave as juniors or seniors, but the reality is that boys typically drop out the very first year they enter high school. Do you know what it's like being a 16 year-old freshman, reading at a third grade level? It is humiliating, and boys can't wait until their 16th birthday to drop out. Unfortunately, many African American males drop out of school because they are unable to secure the latest designer clothes and shoes. We

33

could reduce the dropout rate if every school instituted an inexpensive uniform policy. Making a bad situation even worse is the student/counselor ratio, which, at many public high schools, consists of 250 students to every one counselor. Very little counseling can be done under that arrangement. African American males could benefit from smaller high schools. Many males become lost in schools with thousands of students. Intensive reading and math classes need to be provided without negative stigmatism.

Every effort must be done to address the significant dropout rate of African American males in ninth grade. It is a state of emergency. Just as I've recommended a fourth grade intervention team, we also need a ninth grade intervention team of motivational specialists that will speak to the needs of African American males.

Critical Subjects

In addition to the three critical grades—kindergarten, fourth, and ninth—there are two critical academic subjects I'd like to mention: **reading** and **algebra.** While race and income are generally believed to be the leading precursors of failure in our society, many research studies have found that illiteracy is the single greatest predictor of crime, poverty, and school dropout levels. [11]
Ninety percent of African American inmates are illiterate. [12] Within the problem is the seed to the solution. If we simply taught African American males how to read, we would have a 90 percent chance of keeping them out of jail.

More than a decade ago, Jonathan Kozol reminded us of the serious illiteracy problem in America in his book *Illiterate America*. With 44 million illiterate individuals in this country, it is clear that the problem transcends race. [13]

A study by the Institute for Literacy found that inmates with an education of eighth grade or less were 10 percent more likely to be rearrested than those with some college education. We're in a state of emergency, and every church, school, community organization, recreational center, and literate adult must be called into action to teach our males how to read.

The Village Foundation, a national nonprofit organization that focuses on the plight of African American men, initiated a three-year national literacy campaign in cooperation with the U.S. Department of Labor. The foundation discovered that the percentage of African American adults with extremely low reading levels is nearly twice that of the general adult population. Nearly 40 percent of African American adults fall in the lowest "prose" literacy level, which measures a person's ability to comprehend printed information written in sentence form. [14] Only 21 percent of the general adult population falls in this category.

According to the report, the situation is far worse for young African American males who routinely score 12 to 17 points lower than young African American females on all literacy inventories. Nationally, eighth grade males on the "prose" level literacy scale are 10 percent below the national average and 13 percent below the White average. [15]

However, numerous studies have shown that education reduces the rate of recidivism. An Illinois study found that inmates with an education of eighth grade or less were 10 percent more likely to be rearrested than those with some college education, according to the National Institute for Literacy. [16]

The U.S. Department of Education's 1998 national reading report card for students in the fourth, eighth, and twelfth grades showed a stark difference between Black boys' and White boys' reading ability. In each grade level Black boys scored between 29 and 33 points, or 2.5 to 3.5 grade levels, below their White male counterparts. [17] The National Institutes of Health consider the nation's reading problem so pernicious that researchers have labeled it a major threat to public health.

Nearly a half-century ago Rudolph Flesch wrote *Why Johnny Can't Read*. Two decades later he wrote the sequel *Why Johnny Still Can't Read*. The reason why Johnny and Willie can't read is because they cannot decode words. Good readers are able to sound words out phonetically. Several decades ago American schools moved from the phonetic approach to reading to the sight approach.

In the sight approach, a picture is shown with the relevant word below. For example, a picture of a dog is shown with the word "dog" below the picture. The assumption is that children will learn how to read by correlating pictures and words together. Repetition is often used; as a child sees a word time and again, the greater his chance of mastering the word. See Dick run, see Jane run. They both run, they run again, and run and run and run. At some point Willie will know that the word in question is "run."

The sight approach ensures that words are memorized—but not decoded. Thus, this approach has its limits. With the phonetic approach to reading, however, there is no word that you cannot pronounce once you master basic phonetic tools. When children are taught to sound out words, they have no problem pronouncing my name, Jawanza Kunjufu. The sight approach would not help a student pronounce my name. Only phonics could do that.

Many schools say they use phonics, but how often? Ironically, phonics is usually used in remedial reading programs. If phonics is the best approach in remedial reading, then why not just use phonics in the earlier grades? Might the answer be found in the fact that publishers make more money with the sight approach to reading and that phonics is more labor intensive and requires more work from teachers?

While I remain a phonics advocate, recent research has forced me to qualify my position. Phonics is ideal for left-brain thinkers along with reading aloud. It is not the best approach for right-brain thinkers. These students need to see the whole picture and prefer reading silently so they can better create the images. Right brain thinkers are excellent speed-readers. [18] Teachers should be well trained in both methods so that they can truly meet the diverse learning needs of their students.

Schools that have been successful at improving the reading scores of African American students have not only placed greater emphasis on phonics, but more of the school day is allocated toward reading. They give incentives for their student's reading performance, e.g., the class that reads the most books receives prizes. Dixon School in Chicago is a perfect example of what can be done in spite of the demographics that our children endure. Dixon students primarily come from low-income homes in which fathers are MIA (missing in action). Dixon School is not only one of the most high-achieving schools in Chicago, but in the entire state of Illinois. Seventy-two percent of the students there read above grade level. [19]

Nationwide, only 10 percent of Americans who are illiterate are being served. If we're in a state of emergency and the National Institutes of Health believe illiteracy is a major threat to the nation's public health, then the government must allocate more money to literacy programs. Literacy programs are much more cost effective, and humane, than prisons.

I am reminded of Dr. Ben Carson. In spite of being raised in a home that was low-income and fatherless, he learned to read. His mother made him turn off the television to read a book and write a report. Ben Carson soared and is now considered one of the best pediatric neurosurgeons in the world. I am convinced that Ben Carson's success began with becoming literate.

The second greatest subject that I believe has a significant impact on African American males is algebra. It is the gate keeping subject to college. Algebra is the subject that helps develop critical thinking skills. Affluent families in America ensure that their children receive algebra between fourth and seventh grades. Unfortunately, the least in our society may not receive algebra until tenth or eleventh grade. Possibly the reason African American males drop out in ninth grade is because they never took an algebra class. For an African American male student who has done poorly in school, even if they graduate, they may not be eligible for algebra until their junior or senior year.

Seventy-five percent of African American college students take remedial math classes. Many African American college students think that they got over in high school by taking a minimal number of classes. They now have to spend valuable time and money in either junior or senior college for something they should have received for free in elementary or high school.

The Village Foundation found that the problem is worse for quantitative literacy, which measures a person's ability to process numeric information. Forty-six percent of African American adults scored in the lowest level in this category; the national average was 22 percent. In the category of document literacy (the ability to understand documents that use both words and numbers to communicate a meaning), 43 percent of African American adults scored in the lowest level; the national average was 23 percent. [20]

In our highly technological economy, an understanding of algebra is imperative because computer-programming languages are based on algebraic formulas. Understand algebra and you'll understand computers and technology in general. Sixty percent of new jobs require technological skills that are possessed by only 22 percent of the workforce. In the year 2000, 350,000 computer-programming positions could not be filled by American workers, which meant that foreigners had to be recruited. How unfortunate that a vast majority of the 1.3 million incarcerated African American males were not taught algebra.

Robert Moses has done a tremendous job in addressing the plight of African Americans in the field of algebra. He is the founder of the Algebra Project and the very significant book *Radical Equations*. He spearheaded a movement to have the Algebra Project implemented in schools nationwide. Moses believes that just as we had a burning passion in the civil rights era for the right to vote and for literacy, we need that same passion to ensure that we master algebra.

In *Radical Equations*, Moses teaches that in simple math the question is "how many?" In algebra, however, the question is "which way?" An integer line, going from negative to positive, forms the basis of direction in algebra. The beauty of Moses' approach is that prior to becoming immersed in numbers you are taught *how* to frame a problem. Often critical thinking is about knowing how to ask the right questions.

Research in five Alabama elementary schools demonstrated the effectiveness of the Algebra Project during a three-year project, beginning the fall of 1993. Three schools formed the experimental group and two schools served as the control group. The experimental group received instruction using Algebra Project pedagogy. The control group received traditional instruction. Control schools included predominately White, Westhills, one of Bessemer's top elementary schools, and Abrams, a school whose students come from the poorest segment of the Black community.

Heart School was in the experimental group. Predominately Black with a large portion of its students drawn from poor families in Bessemer, Heart did five points better than Abrams on standardized math tests during the first year of the study. Still, Heart lagged 20 points behind Westhills. The next year Heart's scores remained constant. Abrams did better than usual and Westhills dropped 14 points. By 1998, Westhills was back up to its usual range of 59 points, but Heart now had the best mathematics score in the city with 62 points. Children from the lowest socioeconomic group were outperforming middle and upper class White kids at the flagship school. [21] I strongly recommend that every school district implement the Algebra Project in the fourth grade.

I also want to emphasize the great work of Freeman Hrabowski III at the University of Maryland. Nationally, African Americans represent 91 percent of the NBA starters but only 1.5 percent of the engineers, doctors, computer programmers, dentists, and accountants. Many African American males believe they are better in music than math, sports than science, and rap than reading. Hrabowski identified African American males who scored well mathematically on the SAT and admitted them to the university's engineering program.

Unfortunately, in the past many African American males did not remain in the engineering program for many reasons, including lack of mentoring and peer support. The program is called the Meyerhoff Scholar Program, named after Robert and Jane Meyerhoff. The Meyerhoffs are philanthropists interested in changing the NBA-engineering disparity. The first program began in the fall of 1989 and included 19 African American male college students whose scores ranged between 600 and 800 on the math component of the SAT.

The program has had tremendous success in increasing the number of African American males graduates. More importantly, it has encouraged them to pursue doctorate degrees in mathematics and engineering. Clearly, if African American males have a peer group that reinforces academic achievement and a mentoring program that reinforces a positive value system, then they can reach their full potential. Every college in America should implement a similar program.

Marilyn Ross, author of *Success Factors of Young African American Males at a Historically Black College*, looked at a control group of African American males at Florida Memorial College. Her conclusions reinforce Hrabowski's findings. African American males thrive in nurturing environments that are filled with role models and positive peer pressure. Every college needs a chapter of Student African American Brotherhood (SAAB). It is a critical mistake for us to think that only children in primary and intermediate grades need nurturing, self-esteem, bonding, mentoring, role model, and motivational programs. In a society driven by White male supremacy, we must also meet the spiritual, social, and academic needs of African American males in college. The following chart illuminates African American males pursuit of a college education.

State of Emergency
We _Must_ Save African American Males

Where are the "Brothers?"

Enrollment Numbers

Top 100 Black Male Undergraduate Enrollments - Degrees Fall 1999 Preliminary

Rank	Institution	State	Total Men	Black Men	% Black
1	FLORIDA A&M UNIVERSITY	FL	4539	4176	92%
2	SOUTHERN UNIV. AND A & M COLLEGE	LA	3320	3183	96%
3	MOREHOUSE COLLEGE	GA	3012	2972	99%
4	NORTH CAROLINA A&T STATE UNIV.	NC	3195	2833	89%
5	CUNY NY CITY TECHNICAL COLLEGE	NY	5456	2439	45%
6	TENNESSEE STATE UNIVERSITY	TN	2686	2223	83%
7	MORGAN STATE UNIVERSITY	MD	2357	2221	94%
8	NORFOLK STATE UNIVERSITY	VA	2376	2118	89%
9	JACKSON STATE UNIVERSITY	MS	2173	2103	97%
10	PRAIRIE VIEW A & M UNIVERSITY	TX	2270	2085	92%
11	ALABAMA STATE UNIVERSITY	AL	2073	1938	93%
12	ALABAMA A & M UNIVERSITY	AL	2117	1856	88%
13	HAMPTON UNIVERSITY	VA	1981	1801	91%
14	GRAMBLING STATE UNIVERSITY	LA	1862	1782	96%
15	TEXAS SOUTHERN UNIVERSITY	TX	2007	1732	86%
16	HOWARD UNIVERSITY	DC	2211	1689	76%
17	WAYNE STATE UNIVERSITY	MI	7257	1639	23%
18	SOUTH CAROLINA STATE UNIV.	SC	1701	1602	94%
19	UNIVERSITY OF MEMPHIS	TN	6417	1554	24%
20	TEMPLE UNIVERSITY	PA	7563	1553	21%
21	GEORGIA STATE UNIVERSITY	GA	6347	1498	24%
22	UNIV. OF THE DIST. OF COLUMBIA	DC	2006	1489	74%
23	UNIV. OF MARYLAND-COLLEGE PARK	MD	12704	1463	12%
24	GEORGIA SOUTHERN UNIVERSITY	GA	5984	1438	24%
25	VIRGINIA STATE UNIVERSITY	VA	1491	1400	94%
26	FLORIDA INTERNATIONAL UNIV.	FL	11427	1380	12%
27	BENEDICT COLLEGE	SC	1360	1358	100%
28	UNIV. OF HOUSTON-UNIV. PARK	TX	11478	1323	12%
29	NORTH CAROLINA CENTRAL UNIV.	NC	1484	1322	89%
30	CHICAGO STATE UNIVERSITY	IL	1496	1304	87%
31	UNIV. OF ARKANSAS AT PINE BLUFF	AR	1347	1258	93%
32	CUNY CITY COLLEGE	NY	4028	1241	31%
33	DEVRY INSTITUTE OF TECHNOLOGY	GA	1691	1193	71%
34	SOUTHERN IL UNIV.-CARBONDALE	IL	10181	1189	12%
35	FLORIDA STATE UNIVERSITY	FL	11564	1174	10%
36	UNIV. OF CINCINNATI-MAIN CAMPUS	OH	10557	1157	11%
37	FAYETTEVILLE STATE UNIVERSITY	NC	1476	1122	76%
38	NC STATE UNIVERSITY AT RALEIGH	NC	12804	1104	9%
39	CLARK ATLANTA UNIVERSITY	GA	1105	1101	100%
40	EASTERN MICHIGAN UNIVERSITY	MI	7194	1083	15%
41	OHIO STATE UNIV.-MAIN CAMPUS	OH	18703	1079	6%
42	UNIV. OF MARYLAND-UNIV. COLLEGE	MD	4991	1077	22%
43	UNIV. OF S. CAROLINA AT COLUMBIA	SC	6987	1059	15%
44	MICHIGAN STATE UNIVERSITY	MI	15853	1058	7%
45	BOWIE STATE UNIVERSITY	MD	1199	1054	88%
46	TUSKEGEE UNIVERSITY	AL	1062	1038	98%
47	VIRGINIA COMMONWEALTH UNIV.	VA	6443	1030	16%
48	BETHUNE COOKMAN COLLEGE	FL	1122	1027	92%
49	FORT VALLEY STATE UNIVERSITY	GA	1043	988	95%
50	OLD DOMINION UNIVERSITY	VA	5775	976	17%
51	UNIV. OF LOUISIANA AT LAFAYETTE	LA	6515	969	15%
52	SOUTHERN UNIV. AT NEW ORLEANS	LA	1079	959	89%
53	CUNY BERNARD M BARUCH COLLEGE	NY	5466	954	17%
54	UNIVERSITY OF SOUTH FLORIDA	FL	11063	950	9%
55	ALCORN STATE UNIVERSITY	MS	968	945	98%
56	CUNY BROOKLYN COLLEGE	NY	3927	945	24%
57	ALBANY STATE UNIVERSITY	GA	981	934	95%
58	MISSISSIPPI STATE UNIVERSITY	MS	7146	931	13%
59	UNIV. OF AKRON MAIN CAMPUS	OH	8021	898	11%
60	UNIV. OF MD-EASTERN SHORE	MD	1168	894	77%

Graduation Rate

Black Male Baccalaureate in All 'Disciplines

Rank	Institution	State	No. of Degrees
1	FLORIDA A&M UNIVERSITY	FL	489
2	MOREHOUSE COLLEGE	GA	482
3	NORTH CAROLINA A&T STATE UNIV.	NC	350
4	SOUTHERN UNIV. AND A & M COLLEGE	LA	347
5	HOWARD UNIVERSITY	DC	29
6	GRAMBLING STATE UNIVERSITY	LA	275
7	SOUTHERN IL UNIV.-CARBONDALE	IL	273
8	HAMPTON UNIVERSITY	VA	260
9	TENNESSEE STATE UNIVERSITY	TN	252
10	NORFOLK STATE UNIVERSITY	VA	250
11	SOUTH CAROLINA STATE UNIV.	SC	240
12	UNIV. OF MARYLAND-COLLEGE PARK	MD	224
13	PRAIRIE VIEW A & M UNIVERSITY	TX	224
14	JACKSON STATE UNIVERSITY	MS	216
15	MORGAN STATE UNIVERSITY	MD	211
16	ALABAMA STATE UNIVERSITY	AL	191
17	ALABAMA A & M UNIVERSITY	AL	190
18	NORTH CAROLINA CENTRAL UNIV.	NC	190
19	FLORIDA INTERNATIONAL UNIV.	FL	188
20	UNIV. OF MARYLAND-UNIV. COLLEGE	MD	184
21	UNIVERSITY OF FLORIDA	FL	180
22	CHICAGO STATE UNIVERSITY	IL	179
23	GEORGIA STATE UNIVERSITY	GA	177
24	FLORIDA STATE UNIVERSITY	FL	176
25	UNIV. OF S. CAROLINA AT COLUMBIA	SC	170
26	VIRGINIA STATE UNIVERSITY	VA	70
27	ALCORN STATE UNIVERSITY	MS	168
28	WAYLAND BAPTIST UNIVERSITY	TX	168
29	SAINT LEO UNIVERSITY	FL	167
30	BOWIE STATE UNIVERSITY	MD	167
31	TEMPLE UNIVERSITY	PA	165
32	UNIV. OF MICHIGAN-ANN ARBOR	MI	154
33	FAYETTEVILLE STATE UNIVERSITY	NC	154
34	MICHIGAN STATE UNIVERSITY	MI	153
35	RUTGERS UNIV.-NEW BRUNSWICK	NJ	148
36	TEXAS SOUTHERN UNIVERSITY	TX	148
37	GEORGIA SOUTHERN UNIVERSITY	GA	147
38	UNIV. OF MARYLAND-EASTERN SHORE	MD	146
39	NC STATE UNIVERSITY AT RALEIGH	NC	146
40	PARK UNIVERSITY	MO	144
41	CUNY CITY COLLEGE	NY	144
42	TUSKEGEE UNIVERSITY	AL	142
43	DEVRY INSTITUTE OF TECH-DECATUR	GA	141
44	CUNY BERNARD M BARUCH COLLEGE	NY	141
45	CUNY YORK COLLEGE	NY	141
46	UNIVERSITY OF MEMPHIS	TN	141
47	CUNY J. J. COLL. CRIMINAL JUSTICE	NY	137
48	OHIO STATE UNIV.-MAIN CAMPUS	OH	136
49	CLARK ATLANTA UNIVERSITY	GA	135
50	UNIV. OF SOUTHERN MISSISSIPPI	MS	135
51	UNIV. OF NC AT CHARLOTTE	NC	130
52	U OF PHOENIX-SOUTHERN CA CAMPUS	CA	130
53	MISSISSIPPI VALLEY STATE UNIV.	MS	129
54	UNIV. OF CALIFORNIA-LOS ANGELES	CA	128
55	UNIV. OF CENTRAL FLORIDA	FL	126
56	CUNY BROOKLYN COLLEGE	NY	125
57	VIRGINIA COMMONWEALTH UNIV.	VA	125
58	UNIV. OF VIRGINIA-MAIN CAMPUS	VA	125
59	UNIV. OF IL AT URBANA-CHAMPAIGN	IL	121
60	DELAWARE STATE UNIVERSITY	DE	118

SOURCE: U.S DEPT. OF EDUCATION

Special Education

I often wonder why it's called "special" education. After children matriculate through a special education program, are they returned to mainstream classrooms at grade level? What did schools do with "bad" Black boys before Public Law 194 created special education in 1964? What did African American teachers do with hyperactive African American male students in a one-room school shack with 40 students and a leaky roof? I often wonder how the late Chief Justice Thurgood Marshall would have felt, half a century after the 1954 Brown vs. Topeka decision, about the return to highly segregated tracking and special education programs.

How do we evaluate special education? Seventy-five percent of children who were diagnosed with Attention Deficit Disorder (ADD) are adults also suffering from ADD. Six percent of all children, or six million children, are in special education. There has been a 42 percent increase in special education placements over the past decade. As a result, special education has become a $40 billion industry.

When White America catches a cold, Black America catches the flu. African American children are 17 percent of the children in public schools, but represent almost 40 percent of children placed in special education. A study conducted by Tom Parrish of the American Institute of Research indicates that the United States average for over-identification of African Americans in the area of Emotional Disturbance is 1.92. African American males are placed in special education almost three times as much as girls. [22]

Given these statistics, it is clear that schools have failed in the education of African American males. Is there a school in America that places more African American females in special education than African American males? Ironically, in Germany and Japan, there are more female students in special education than males. In general, the percentage of students in special education is far less than ours.

There are more male teachers in Germany and Japan than in the U.S. Might that explain why there are more females in special education than males in those countries? Could it be that some people believe that different is synonymous with deficient? Are African American males disproportionately placed in special education because there are so few African American male teachers in the U.S.? White females are placed in special education the least. Why? Because White females dominate as teachers in this country? Public Law 194 was never intended to be a dumping ground for African American male students, nor was it intended to be the new form of tracking. The National Medical Association believes that 20 percent of African Americans are over diagnosed and erroneously placed in special education. [23] In my opinion, that is a conservative estimate.

I mentioned earlier that there are five types of adults in our classrooms and that there are too many referral agents and custodians. Ninety percent of children referred are placed in special ed. Twenty percent of the staff makes 80 percent of the referrals. [24]

In, *The Color of Discipline*, produced by the Indiana Education Policy Center, the authors note that African American over representation in special education classes decreased as the representation of African Americans in school faculties increased. [25] They suggested the possibility of bias in the referral process.

The Miseducation of African American Males

The discrimination that has taken place in special education reached Congress, and the Individuals with Disabilities Educational Act was passed in 1997. The Act attempts to evaluate special education, which over the past decade has increased by 42 percent. Four million of the six million children in special education have been classified as ADD. Schools received $4.3 billion for special education students. Could schools be financially encouraged to place students in special education? Unfortunately, African Americans are 41 percent of special education students, but only seven percent of gifted and talented students.

Since 1956, there's been a *600 percent* increase in the usage of Ritalin. Ninety percent of ADD children take Ritalin. The remaining uses Adderall, Dexedrine, or Cylert. [26] The American Psychiatric Association and Ciby Geigy the manufacturer of Ritalin are under investigation for possible conspiracy. By increasing the popularity of this drug, both parties have increased their coffers. The Congressional Act is designed to put pressure on school districts to look at the disproportionate percentage of all children in special education, specifically children of color, who are prescribed drugs. They also recommend that tests should encompass the learning styles and culture of children.

Let me describe a typical scenario. An enthusiastic Black boy entering kindergarten loves learning and is asking all kinds of questions. Due to his lack of maturity, short attention span, high energy level, and low-level gross motor skills, he is unfortunately referred to special education. Many social workers and psychologists tell me that it is very difficult to convince a teacher who has made the referral to change her mind. I mentioned earlier that 90 percent of referrals are placed.

State of Emergency
We <u>Must</u> Save African American Males

The most important meeting of a child's life is scheduled for 12:00 noon, the Individual Educational Plan (IEP). While the meeting is scheduled for 12:00, four professionals arrive at 11:30—the principal, psychologist, social worker, and teacher. At 12:00, a low-income single parent arrives for the meeting. She feels like she has been talked about. The dye has been cast, and the decision has already been made.

We are losing our boys one by one. We are in a state of emergency. Before parents enter another IEP meeting, they should be well armed. They need to have legal representation; if they cannot afford it, they should contact the NAACP, the Legal Aid Society, Black Social Workers, or the Black Psychologist Association to represent them. Mothers should always have a man present at an IEP meeting. Most schools respond better in his presence. And last but not least, they should provide a videotape of their son reading a book, playing dominos, checkers, concentration, or some mental exercise in excess of 20 minutes. Parents need to document that their children can learn under better classroom management conditions. Parents must also reduce time allocated for television and video games.

I do not accept that African American children are only 17 percent of American students, but 41 percent of special education students. I do not accept that 80 percent of African American special education referrals are male. That statistic alone necessitates a state of emergency.

I believe the problem is not with bad Black boys, but with poor classroom management. Isn't it ironic that the year when Willie was with a teacher or a coach he was not labeled ADD, but the year when he was with a referral agent or custodian he was labeled special education? I wonder how many left-brain thinkers are labeled ADD? Unions protect referral agents and custodians. Who is protecting African American males in this state of emergency?

In my earlier book, *Satan I'm Taking Back My Health*, and in the tremendous work of Dr. Mary Block in the book *No More Ritalin*, we discuss how poor nutrition creates problems in our children. Forty percent of ADD children have a nutritional deficiency. [27] I commend Dr. Mary Block, a parent who was called to one of those IEP meetings. While Block is neither an African American nor poor, she represents many White families in America who are also affected by the misdiagnosis of their children. Mary Block was a layperson who decided to go to medical school and become a doctor so she could fight for the rights of her children. I pray that parents do not need to become doctors and lawyers to adequately represent their children in the IEP. Instead I would encourage all parents facing this problem to read our books. They discuss the following:

If 40 percent of ADD children have a nutritional deficiency, is Ritalin the correct prescription? The average American is consuming 155 pounds of sugar annually. Have you ever seen a sugar-free school? Before we label another child hyperactive and ADD, we may want to reduce, if not eliminate, sugar from the school diet.

Some ADD-labeled children are suffering from mineral and essential oil deficiencies. In addition, many children are suffering from hypoglycemia, allergies (to dairy, peanuts, artificial coloring, MSG, and preservatives), or problems with their thyroid gland. Many children need hearing and visual exams. Dr. Block documented that 69 percent or students labeled hyperactive, suffered from ear infections. [28] Several medical studies have concluded that when nutrition is improved there is a reduction in ADD placement ranging from 54 to 86 percent. Caffeine and simple carbohydrates should also be eliminated.

Dr. Block and I also agree that Ritalin can cause a loss of appetite, irreversible brain damage, nervousness, insomnia, dizziness, headaches, high blood pressure, and lethargy. Nationwide, groups are rising up and addressing the issue. One group is called Parents Against Ritalin. Are doctors being trigger-happy and prescribing Ritalin too quickly? Is it because the previously cited factors that may contribute to ADD require more time to access? Are doctors not considering the lifetime implications of Ritalin usage?

Christina Sommers in her book *The War Against Boys* points out that recess, the one time during the school day when boys can legitimately engage in rowdy play, is now under siege and may soon be a thing of the past. In 1998, Atlanta eliminated recess in all elementary schools. In Philadelphia, school officials have replaced traditional recess with socialized recess, in which children are assigned structured, carefully monitored activities. The *New York Times* reported that the Cleveland Avenue Grammar School, housed in a handsome brick building, was built two years ago without a playground. [29] The move to eliminate recess has aroused little notice and even less opposition. To label children hyperactive, prescribe them Ritalin, and feed them sugar while forbidding recess and movement in the classroom borders on criminality. Lack of exercise is a major contributor to children labeled ADD.

It is also criminal for African American parents to welcome their child being placed in special education for financial reasons. Some parents illegally receive Supplemental Security Income (SSI). This income should only be provided when a child is blind, deaf, suffering from cerebral palsy, Down's syndrome, muscular dystrophy, HIV, amputation, or significant mental deficiency.

Zero tolerance, however, is perhaps the most criminal policy of all. Could you have lived under a zero tolerance policy? Let those who have not sinned throw the first stone, and remember in the biblical story that the elders walked away first. The elders are implementing and enforcing zero tolerance on young, innocent children, primarily African American males. Nationwide, African American children are 17 percent of the children in public schools but represent 32 percent of the students suspended. One of every four African American males will be suspended. In 1998, 87,000 were expelled. In 1974, 1.7 million students were suspended; in 2000 that figure was close to four million. While school crime was down 40 percent between 1995 and 2000, suspension and expulsion rates have increased drastically. [30]

In a later chapter on prisons we will talk about the tremendous influence of the media. Parents are being led by the media to believe that schools are not safe. As a result of the media's tremendous emphasis on Santee, Columbine, Oregon, Kentucky, Arkansas, and Flint, many parents have an unrealistic and inaccurate view of schools. Columbine is the anomaly, not the norm. But as a result of media sensationalism, there has been a knee-jerk reaction in our society, and African American males are paying the price. Black boys are not going into schools shooting victims randomly. Can you imagine if African American males had been the perpetrators in Santee, Columbine and other "all American" schools?

Several African American males were throwing peanuts at each other on a school bus in Mississippi. They were taken to jail. The charges were dropped, but they lost their bus privileges. They lived 30 miles from the school and without bus privileges they had to drop out. Many of the boys had college aspirations. A five-year-old African American male wore an offensive Halloween costume to school and was expelled. A six-year-old boy had a toenail clipper; it was ruled a weapon and he was expelled. A fourth grade student brought a toy gun to school; that was also viewed as a weapon and he was expelled. A fifth grader took two shaving blades from a student and was turning them in to the principal, but was accused of possession and expelled. A seventh grader was expelled for sniffing Whiteout. [31]

Jesse Jackson Sr. brought national attention to zero tolerance when several boys in Decatur, Illinois, were fighting, without guns or knives. No one was hurt, but six males were expelled. Not only were they expelled; they were not given any opportunity to attend an educational institution to receive credit.

Decatur, Illinois, is not an anomaly. Only 24 states provide educational opportunities for students who are expelled, and many of those facilities are inadequate. In Massachusetts, African Americans are 20 percent of the population, but 54 percent of students expelled. In Arizona, African Americans have a 22 times greater chance of being expelled. In Austin, San Francisco, Denver, L.A., Durham, Providence, Columbia, South Carolina, African Americans have a three times greater chance of being expelled. In Chicago in 1992 only 14 students were expelled, but in 1999 that figure swelled to 737. [32]

The Miseducation of African American Males

It has become such a state of emergency in Raleigh Durham, North Carolina, that the NAACP halted the school board meeting when it was reported that 70 percent of African American males drop out. The American Bar Association has a resolution against that zero tolerance. [33]

In Russell Skiba's *The Color of Discipline*, the researchers wanted to scientifically look at three factors: race, income, and behavior. America still believes that until you can document racism quantitatively, it does not exist. This study proved beyond a shadow of a doubt that race was the driving factor in the disproportionate percentage of African American males being suspended, expelled, and placed in special education. Their research negated the fact that income is the major factor in the determination of school suspensions and expulsions. The disproportionate percentage of African American males that were victims of zero tolerance transcended income.

Some educators that are still in a state of denial would say the reason why African American males are suspended and expelled more than other students is because they commit more infractions. Again, this exhaustive study done in several settings, including integrated schools, documents that there were not a greater number of infractions by African American students, but there were differences in how school personnel responded. The report illustrates the ambiguity between subjective and objective responses. We know that when Whites are pulled over by the police they receive a warning; when African Americans are pulled over, we receive a ticket. The report illustrates that White behaviors were in more extreme categories, including possession of a weapon, fighting, and smoking. Yet, even those major infractions often did not generate suspension or expulsion.

In contrast, disciplinary responses to "infractions" committed by African Americans were purely subjective. Black kids behaving according to the dictates of their culture were perceived by teachers as threatening, noisy, and disrespectful. Hanging out with friends was called "loitering." Many teachers are uncomfortable and intimidated by Black dialect, shoulder shrugging, sagging, baggy clothes, and direct eye contact. Richard Majors describes this in the book *Cool Pose.*

The report goes on to document that strong principals create a climate that encourages students. The atmosphere is not punitive, but educational and developmental. There are fewer student suspensions and expulsions. Ironically, there could be two schools in the same neighborhood with similar demographics, yet the rate of African American male suspensions and expulsions could be completely opposite.

Classroom management is another critical factor in the treatment of Black males. The report recommends that teachers receive more in-service training on how to respond appropriately to different cultural behaviors. For example, many teachers are not aware that the "dozens," "signifying," "cracking," and "ranking" are designed to avoid physical fighting. These verbal rituals allow boys to verbally jockey. There is a very good chance that after "the dozens," they will then become the best of friends and the loser will probably use the winner's lines in his next verbal skirmish.

What are we thinking as a society when we expel a child for two years and not provide him with the opportunity to earn credits and ultimately to graduate? What roles will that person play in our society? We are experiencing a state of emergency and the disproportionate percentage of African American males suspended and expelled must be reduced.

Is there a relationship between Ritalin and cocaine? Between special education and suspension? Between zero tolerance and prison? Are schools designed to provide prisons with fodder? To circumvent the disproportionate percentage of African American males suspended and expelled include improving school climate, I recommend better classroom management, and peer judicial due process. I also recommend the following:

1.   School districts must appoint a separate board to determine expulsion. Decatur's school board voted down racial lines, and those boys never stood a chance. African American males are suspended and expelled three times greater than White students. [34] The expulsion board members should reflect the culture, community, and race of the defendants. The future of African American males cannot remain in the hands of "out of touch," insensitive Whites.
2.   Every state must provide quality educational alternatives for students who have been expelled.
3.   A moratorium should be placed on any school district that is not in compliance with the percentage of African American students in their district. Therefore, if African Americans are only 17 percent of the students in the district and their suspension or expulsion figure surpasses that number, then a moratorium would be placed on that school district. States should reduce funding if schools are not in compliance.
4.   Every school district must train their staff in Dr. King's method of nonviolent techniques. My company, African American Images, has developed a Dr. King classroom that teaches children how to resolve conflict through nonviolence. I am always amazed at how schools love

Martin Luther King on the third Monday in January, but hate him for his beliefs. Dr. King was far more than a dreamer. He was a scholar, a preacher, an author, a minister, and a civil rights activist. His fundamental belief was nonviolence. Today we have boys who will kill you because you brushed up against them, stepped on their shoe, or said something offensive to them. They need Dr. King's approach more than ever today.

5.   I also recommend the Malcolm X in-house suspension class. When African American boys are suspended, they must be given constructive activities and on school grounds. It makes no sense to send children home. That's a vacation!

Let's keep boys in the building and implement the same strategies Elijah Muhammad used with Malcolm X. Males with a submissive personality are easily influenced by peer pressure. In contrast, males with a domineering personality lack tack when interacting with authority figures. In both the King and Malcolm classes, we look for these personality traits and attempt to steer males toward a proper balance. More will be provided on the Malcolm X class in the Solution chapter.

Let's now look at the impact the miseducation of African American males has had on their ability to economically compete in the new economy.

**TATE**

OF

**MERGENCY**

THE ECONOMIC SYSTEM

We live in a country that is capitalistic and patriarchal. It is very difficult for man to live in a capitalistic country without capital. It is also very difficult for a man to live in a country that is patriarchal and not be the head of the house. It is difficult living in a patriarchal country with low self-esteem. It is very challenging living an unproductive life in America. Most African American men define themselves from a Eurocentric perspective. The definition of manhood is based on capital accumulation. This is expressed primarily in clothes, jewelry, appliances, cars, and houses. Unfortunately, that is the order in which many African Americans demonstrate their level of worth. Whites reverse that order to create wealth.

Nihilism is a feeling of worthlessness. It can cause a deep level of depression and frustration, which is expressed in a number of different ways, but primarily through homicide and suicide. Why do Black men kill Black men? If they are such good killers, why don't they kill everybody? People without a future are dangerous. Humans without goals have nothing to lose. In the movie *Juice*, Tupac demonstrated that you kill people who look just like you when you hate yourself.

In *Countering the Conspiracy to Destroy Black Boys,* I described entropy. It is primarily a technological term that is used to describe the utilization of parts in a machine. When the part is no longer functional, not only does it damage the larger machine, it also destroys itself. The same is true of humans. If African American males do not feel productive, if they lack capital, they cause havoc and chaos in the larger community. They damage themselves.

We are in a state of emergency. Nihilism and entropy are at all time highs among African American males. Suicide is on the rise in the African American community; there has been a 146 percent increase over the past decade. Twenty-five per 100,000 African American males are victims of suicide. [35]

Forticide is a hybrid of homicide and suicide. Many times the police are quick to declare a homicide as being gang related when in reality it was a suicide mission. Two males who hated themselves wanted to die. They placed themselves in a situation where it was two against 20 others. They understood going into the mission they were going to die. Was it homicide, suicide, or forticide? We are in a state of emergency. Homicide, suicide, forticide, nihilism, and entropy are at all time highs in the Black male community. We must find ways to empower African American males.

Two blue-collar males are laid off. The first male suffers nihilism; he abuses his wife, children, and himself. He drinks and smokes more. (You would think he'd drink and smoke less.) I ask my male readers the following question: How long could you be unemployed and maintain your present level of self-esteem? When I speak on this subject I often ask the females in the audience how long they would stay with their unemployed husband? It takes a certain type of woman to stay in a relationship with an unemployed man.

The Economic System

Two books that raised my consciousness were, *Who Needs the Negro* by Sidney Wilhelm and Sam Yette's *The Choice*. Both raised the question, why were Africans brought to this country? The answer was to work. Does that reason exist today? The answer is no. The question becomes, what does America do with a people, specifically African American males, who are no longer needed? The plantations and farms have all been worked. The factories have closed and those jobs have been exported to Mexico City and South Korea. African American males are needed only to populate prisons and play in stadiums.

Recently we have seen men do both. Rae Carruth illustrates nihilism with the killing of the mother of his child and the permanent damage of his child. More will be said about Rae Carruth in the chapter on fatherlessness.

In the previous chapter on education, we documented the impact miseducation has on African American males. How will a man produce if he is illiterate, especially in our technological society? What are the economic options for an 18-year-old high school graduate who barely passed the minimum exit exam?

Many of our youth suffering from nihilism and entropy believe their options are limited to the NBA, rap, military service, a job at UPS, a minimum wage job, or selling drugs. That's the extent of Black economic development for African American males.

Why was there so much concern from the White media about teenagers going pro in the NBA? Did I miss the discussion about White male and female teenagers going pro in baseball, hockey, tennis, golf etc.? How can White society be so concerned about the future of African American males in the NBA and be disinterested in African American males being disproportionately placed in special education, expulsion, and prisons? Is White society being disingenuous? Is the real issue that five African American male high school graduates and numerous other college students left early because they understood capitalism and chose a guaranteed multi-year, multi-million dollar contract? I wonder how many people reading this would refuse the above and pursue education? We must expand the economic possibilities for our youth. A people that earns $533 billion with two million college graduates, 85,000 churches, 106 Black colleges, and hundreds of wealthy athletes and entertainers should provide better economic options. Claude Anderson in *Powernomics* reminds us that only two percent of college educated African Americans work in Black businesses. He also teaches us is it any wonder why Whites live so well, they keep 100 percent of their income and 97 percent of ours! [36]

The NBA lockout showed us just how displeased owners are at high school graduates like Kevin Garnett earning multi-million, multi-year contracts (Garnett's contact will net him $126 million). There is a lot of discussion around the league about whether high school graduates should be eligible for the NBA. Basketball has become the sports centerpiece. Many African American males play no other sport but basketball. With the success of Allen Iverson, many of our youth believe that they can be as small as 5'9" and still go pro. When I speak to youth around the country I ask them, "What are you going to be doing when you're 30 years of age?" Almost one-half say they'll be playing pro ball in the NBA. I don't discourage them, but every adult needs to explain to youth that the odds of that happening are seven out of a million.

Unfortunately, many of our children believe the chances of becoming an engineer, computer programmer, dentist, doctor, or accountant are seven out of a million. We must help them see that those professions are within their reach. We must expose them to professionals. The spirit of NCAA's Propositions 14, 16, 42 and 48 has the same spirit of special education, zero tolerance, and three strikes. These propositions require a certain GPA and achievement test score to be eligible for a scholarship. The entire burden is borne by the athlete and not by the school system that miseducated them. There is no accountability for schools that have teachers with low expectations, poor classroom management skills, left-brained lesson plans, and an irrelevant curriculum. Many youth believe they have a greater chance of skipping college and going straight into the NBA.

The second option for many of our males is a rap contract. Half of BET's programming seems to feature music videos. We tell youth to learn Standard English so that they can get a good job downtown, taking orders from the White man. Today's youth would rather split verbs and make more money rapping. Youth are really not aware of how difficult it is to become a professional rapper. Nor do they know that five companies control most of the distribution and radio play. As a result, many rappers are paid less than $.25 per CD sale. It is even more unfortunate that many rappers who have begun to earn an adequate income still suffer from nihilism, which is illustrated by their associations. They make more income but possess a ghetto mentality. Why are superstars still hanging with gangsters in bars?

The third option for our youth is the military. "Be all that you can be." Many of our males are trying to graduate from high school for the sole purpose of joining the military. They believe the lie that you can be all you can be. While the military offers college, what percentage complete their education while enlisted? Have you ever asked a military recruiter to provide that percentage? It's as dismal as the graduation rate of African American athletes at colleges and universities. Unfortunately, many mothers believe the military is their best option to teach a young Black male responsibility. The percentages of African American males that receive dishonorable discharges, suffer from alcoholism, and drug abuse are running rampant in the military.

The next option for many of our youth is a minimum wage job. The state of Wisconsin studied the impact of dropping out on male students of all races. Twenty-four percent of African Americans who dropped out were employed. Of the 8,421 dropouts, only 885 were paid a wage adequate to maintain a family. One-half of that number came from those fortunate to work the few remaining manufacturing positions. Seventeen percent of employed African American males live below the poverty line. [37]

There is a distinction between a minimum wage and a living wage. If you make $6 an hour and work 40 hours a week, that's $240 for the week, $960 for the month, and $12,480 for a 52-week year. After taxes, it's $10,000 annually. How do you propose marriage to someone when you're only making $10,000 a year? How do you buy a house, insurance, and raise children with $10,000? Many uneducated and undereducated African American males average even less, because they work part time (20-30 hours per week).

I guess the Fortune 500 and the Trilateral Commission have decided that African American males can make a greater contribution to society by serving as prison fodder. Has society decided that it is better to pay $18,000 to $38,000 to incarcerate them than for them to pay taxes off $10,000? Thirty-four percent of African American males who are single live below the poverty line. Fifty three percent of inmates were earning less than $10,000 before incarceration. [38]

The last option for many of our youth is selling drugs. Unfortunately, many African American males view it as the first option. In a subsequent chapter on drugs, we will give a full analysis of the impact drugs have had on African American males. Suffice to say there is no industry more profitable than the drug industry. When our youth compare a minimum wage job at McDonald's to selling drugs for $1,000.

In Ohio, a study found that in order to discourage males from dealing drugs they would need to earn $15 per hour, work a minimum of 30 hours per week, and have a monthly income of $2,000. [39] In subsequent chapters on drugs and prison, we will document how much money America is willing to spend for drug enforcement and incarceration. Yet this Ohio study documents that for $2,000 a month we can turn suffering African American males from nihilism and entropy into responsible men, husbands, fathers, and taxpayers. Why spend $18,000 to $38,000 to incarcerate males instead of $24,000 to produce responsible, tax-paying citizens?

Integration greatly affected and reduced the village. Once upon a time, brothers and sisters with PhD's and brothers and sisters on ADC lived on the same block. Today, our neighborhoods are concentrated in poverty. While only seven percent of White families live in poverty, more than 30 percent of African Americans live in impoverished neighborhoods. Some African American males live in families where no one works. They live in buildings where no one works. They live on blocks where no one works. Some Black male children live in housing developments that are populated solely with women and children. It's as if the men have gone off to war, but the war is not in Germany, Japan, or Vietnam. The war is in the community. When housing developments of 5,000 people have less than 50 males as permanent residents, we are experiencing a state of emergency. Cincinnati illustrates the complexity. While police brutality is unacceptable, the rash of murders by Black male predators illustrates an impotent community that does not have enough men to police itself.

The critical age range for African American males is 15 to 33. If we can find a way to keep our males safe within this age range we have an excellent chance of saving our families and communities. Homicide and suicide are at their zenith between the ages of 12 and 25. In the last chapter on Solutions, we will talk about some very extreme options to preserve African American males within this age range. This should be the best range for African American males. It should be a time where they are acquiring an education, skills, and building an economic nest.

Other men in America in this age range are soaring economically, but it is diabolically the opposite for African American males. Fifteen to 33 is the most dangerous time period for African American males. Although African American males in this age group are filled with testosterone, ego, intelligence, and vigor, nihilism and entropy are at their most intense. I've already declared the grades that are critical for Black boys. Now I'll go one step further and say that *what an African American male does at 18 will probably determine what he will do for the rest of his life.* We need an African American village to give direction to African American males at 18.

Some African American scholars are trying to lead us to believe that there is a level economic playing field. The research shows there is an economic disparity in Black/White income. An African American male with a high school diploma will only earn $10.56 per hour while a White high school graduate will earn $13.12 per hour. An African American with a college degree will earn $16.53 per hour while a White male with a college degree will earn $21.45 per hour. Only 15 percent of employed African American males attain management or professional positions compared to 30 percent of White males. Thirty-three percent of African American males are employed in the manual labor category.

African American males with college degrees only earn 72 percent of White income. They earn $34,000 in comparison to White males who average $48,000 per year. While the numbers of African American males who have graduated from college have increased over the past three decades, ironically, the income gap widens with educational attainment. When you compare the previous hourly figures of $10.56 to $13.12, African American males earn 80 percent of what White males earn with high school diplomas. When you then look at the college figures of $16.53 to $21.45, African American males only earn 77 percent of what White male college graduates earn. [40]

The following chart shows college attendance by race and gender:

White Males	49%
White Females	51%
Asian Males	54%
Asian Females	46%
Hispanic Males	45%
Hispanic Females	55%
African American Males	37%
African American Females	63%
American Indian Males	30%
American Indian Females	70% [41]

Of the five groups mentioned, only American Indians are worse off than African Americans. Only 37 percent of African American college students are male and even that figure is suspect. If we disaggregate the data via two-year and four-year colleges, graduation rates, and athletes, the disparity would be greater. I speak at approximately 50 colleges per year and in many schools the ratio of Black females to males is much greater than 2:1. I've spoken at some colleges where the ratio was 10:1. We are experiencing a state of emergency.

In the past decade, the economy created 12 million new jobs. Only 700,000 of those jobs did not require a college education. What are African American males to do if they do not possess the skills? Nihilism, entropy, homicide, suicide, and forticide are not acceptable options.

Earlier, I mentioned that 34 percent of African American males who are single live below the poverty line. Research shows that marriage is very beneficial to African American males. They live longer, less chance for unemployment, and greater wages. But remember, it's very difficult to propose marriage to someone when you're earning $6 per hour.

There is much that we can learn from the above. The critical age range is 15 to 33. Marriage can be very beneficial to African American males. Research also shows that if African American males earn a livable wage their divorce rate decreases by eight percent. [42] The million-dollar question is how do we get African American males in this age group to earn a livable wage and marry versus shacking while unemployed, underemployed, addicted, or incarcerated?

I have five answers to that question. They include the Booker T. Washington program, empowerment zones, the Marshall Bill, Kazi, and Ujamaa.

The debate between Booker T. Washington and W.E.B. Dubois must end. It's not about blue collars vs. white collars. The objective is to make yourself economically useful in the current economy. Many of our young people are being discouraged away from the trade industry where plumbers, carpenters, electricians, bricklayers, and the rest are making $18 to $40 per hour, while African Americans with liberal arts degrees are unemployed.

During the UPS strike we discovered just how well those drivers are paid. Two of my college classmates who graduated with education degrees left the field because they could make more money driving a truck or a bus. Please do not misquote me. I am not advocating that we forsake a college education. In the spirit of Maat (an African value system), I'm recommending balance. We must value both blue and white-collar positions. Black leadership in every city must develop blue-collar schools and create entrance into the unions.

Second, we must combine the Marshall Bill and the empowerment zones. After World War II, America helped to restore Germany and Japan through the Marshall Bill. Empowerment zones have had marginal success in addressing the state of emergency in the African American community. Let's merge empowerment zones with the Marshall Bill. I'm proposing that legislation be introduced ensuring that that African Americans receive the same percentage of building contracts as their population. It makes no sense for a building project to take place in the African American community and everyone but African Americans are working on the project.

We've had enough workshops, conferences, and meetings on race relations. Rodney King, it is not about "can we all just get along." It's about sharing power. *Power drives racism.* When Harold Washington was the mayor of Chicago, the city had a $3 billion budget. There were 16 White wards and 34 wards of color. For some strange reason, the 16 White wards were receiving two-thirds of the

$3 billion budget. All Harold Washington wanted to do, in the spirit of Maat, was to give each ward one equal share of the $3 billion budget. Many people in the Black community couldn't understand why the White community was upset with Harold Washington, but that's because many African Americans didn't understand the power struggle. If Harold Washington had been successful, the White community would have lost $1 billion.

I'm very much aware that this legislation is going to be difficult to pass, but we must try. We must remember the success of former Mayor Maynard Jackson in Atlanta who refused to have the airport built without strong African American involvement. In the spirit of Dr. Martin Luther King, we must demand involvement or practice civil disobedience.

Many people specifically youth are critical of the civil rights tactic of marching. They want immediate and substantive remedies. Many critics of the Million Man, Woman, Youth, and Family marches believed that the major beneficiaries were the airlines, hotels, and restaurants. I believe that there's some truth to their criticism, but the major objective of a march is to bring media attention to an issue. Rev. Al Sharpton's march on the Puerto Rican island of Vieques is a perfect illustration. Most people did not know about the bombings and its effect on the indigenous population, prior to the march. As a result of his efforts, and others, President Bush has recommended the halting of the bombs. Marching has been very successful at disrupting construction sites in Black communities where all workers were White. Marching was successful in Cincinnati in the protest against police brutality. The White power structure understood our concern when the business community lost significant sales and could possibly lose tourists and conventions.

But leadership should not rely solely on marches. They are reactionary and illustrate a people without an offensive strategy. Marches illustrate what we are against; building and supporting our institutions reflect what we value.

The last two ideas I discussed in full detail in my book, *Black Economic Solutions for Community Empowerment*. The first program is Kazi. It is a Swahili word for work. It hurts me to drive through the African American community and see intelligent, energetic young African American males being unproductive and hanging on corners with nothing to do. They have been reduced down to a dollar bill in a capitalistic society. If there are no dollars demanding their service, they simply do not work. We need African American leaders to put our people back to work. The Kazi program only requires a good administrator and a computer. We do not need dead presidents, i.e., dollar bills, to be the medium of exchange to employ our people. The Kazi program is based on the African concept of barter. We exchange labor without dollar bills.

An African American male who knows how to paint, cut hair, or any other particular skill would be sent out to provide x number of hours of labor. The administrator would credit his account by that number of hours. When this same man wanted something done for him, his account would be debited. Men are now productive and receiving goods and services for their labor.

The other program is Ujamaa, a Swahili word for cooperative economics. Churches and community organizations across Black America could have groups of 100 or more pool their money. The members would develop business plans, and the one who has the best business plan would receive the money raised that particular night. That person would promise to circulate the dollars among the vendors present. The members would meet the following week or month and would do it again until everyone with a business plan receives the capital necessary to start a business. We would create incubators to share space, staff, and equipment.

Lastly, because we are in a state of emergency, we can no longer afford Black churches depositing $3 billion in White banks on Monday morning. We also cannot afford African American consumers spending 97 percent of their money outside African American businesses. We could put our people back to work if we simply corrected the above two practices. In the following chapter on drugs, we will explore the consequences of our failure.

**TATE**

OF

**MERGENCY**

THE DRUG INDUSTRY

I love statistics. I believe it is important to quantify a problem. The drug industry is massive. Depending on whose research you follow, the sale of drugs annually on the low side is $100 billion and $500 billion on the high side. The war on drugs began in 1971. Over the past three decades America has spent $30 trillion in law enforcement.

It's hard for many people to fathom $1 million much less $30 trillion. What that means is that America is spending $1 trillion per year. That means that every day for the past 30 years America has spent almost $3 billion per day to fight drug addiction. [43]

Throughout this chapter we will raise questions: Is there a war on drugs in America? Are we winning the war? Is there a war on Black men? Have we been good stewards with the money? Could the money have been spent differently? Are there other programs that are more cost effective?

Each year $20 billion of property is stolen by drug users to finance their habit. Thirty percent of all property crime is committed by drug users. I wonder how many televisions, VCRs, stereos, computers, appliances, and valuables my readers have lost to finance this drug industry. Thirty percent of all violent crimes are perpetrated by drug users. Corporate America estimates that $100 billion is lost in productivity. Americans spend $3 billion on drug paraphernalia. [44] I commend community activists and religious leaders who have placed pressure on neighborhood stores, primarily owned by foreigners, to stop selling drug paraphernalia to children. There are 500,000 children in America born drug addicted.

The American school system has a problem educating children, especially children of color who are not addicted. The present school system is not capable of educating the increasing number of children born addicted.

How extensive is drug use in America? There are 106 million Americans who drink alcohol. Imagine that the 1920s prohibition on the sale of alcohol was in effect today. It would be impossible to enforce. There are 57 million Americans who smoke cigarettes. Could America exist with a prohibition on cigarettes with almost 20 percent of the population desirous of smoking?

There are 12 million Americans who use marijuana and 71 million have tried it. Three million Americans use cocaine and 500,000 Americans use heroin. Heroin users have remained constant over the past three decades in spite of the $30 trillion war chest. Seventy percent of nicotine, cocaine, and heroin users are addicted in contrast to only 15 percent of alcohol and marijuana users. There are 15 million hardcore users in America. [45]

Death Rate By Drugs	
8,000	Heroin
15,000	Cocaine
100,000	Alcohol
435,000	Nicotine [46]

The Drug Industry

Drug Users	
106 million	Alcohol
57 million	Smokers
12 million	Marijuana
3 million	Cocaine
500,000	Heroin

One hundred and six million Americans have decided they want to drink liquor. Fifty-seven million Americans have told the government they want to smoke regardless of the Surgeon General's warnings. Many want to smoke marijuana, and there are some interesting arguments to support their desire. Seventy-one million people have tried marijuana, and there are 12 million regular users. Reportedly, no one has ever died from marijuana use. In the year 2000, 700,000 Americans were arrested for marijuana.

The ACLU and the president of the American Bar Association also feel marijuana should be legalized. Interesting, only Western states have allowed marijuana to be used within some legal parameters. Those states include Alaska, California, Nevada, Oregon, Washington, and Arizona. Citizens in the East, Midwest, and Southern regions will either have to consider relocating or convince their legislators. Ironically, one the major reasons marijuana has not been legalized is because of the pharmaceutical industry. They are afraid that the use of marijuana will affect their bottom line. If marijuana was legal, there would be a reduction in demand for legal drugs. The pharmaceutical industry has a very strong lobby; the combination of their lobby and the DEA (Drug Enforcement Association) has prevented the legalization of marijuana.

I have even seen many marijuana advocates misconstrue scripture and take Genesis 1:29 out of context. It reads, "God said, 'See I have given you every herb that yields seed which is on the face of all the earth and every tree whose fruit yields seed. To you it shall be for food'." Many people use that scripture to rationalize their marijuana use. That same argument could be used for cocaine.

There is a difference between using a plant for food and inhaling a plant to create a psychedelic experience.

As a vegetarian and a Christian, I do not use alcohol, nicotine, marijuana, cocaine, or heroin. But putting my personal position aside, if the Drug Enforcement Association and the American public believe they can deny 71 million people who have tried marijuana and would probably like to try it again if it was legal and 12 million who continue regardless of the DEA; they need to reconsider their policy. Marijuana has reached the point of nicotine and alcohol and because it is less addictive, no one has died from it, possesses medical benefits, and because our prison system cannot accommodate 700,000 Americans who have been in possession of marijuana, it is time for America to legalize marijuana. Winning the war on drugs is far more likely against the three million cocaine users and 500,000 heroin users.

What has been the impact of drugs on the Black community? It used to be said that nothing could separate Black mothers from their children. Slavery did not separate Black mothers from their children. Numerous stories throughout history illustrate mothers sold to one state, and the children sold to another, and she went looking for her children. *I now believe that the greatest attack on the Black family was not slavery, but crack cocaine.* I believe this is one of Satan's greatest weapons, and it has had a devastating effect on the African American community.

Addicted mothers will turn tricks in front of their children for crack cocaine. They will deny they have children. In jail and separated from their children, many of these innocent women thought that the man in their life was doing them a favor when they gave them free drugs. The gospel songstress Helen Baylor sang about that in her testimony on the CD *The Live Experience*. Satan can make it feel good and it's free, but it will cost you the rest of your life.

Few Black families have escaped the drug scourge. Almost all of us either have a loved one or someone we know who has been affected by drugs. Thousands of marriages have been destroyed because of drug addiction. There are Black neighborhoods that look like war zones. Property values have deteriorated to all time lows. This is the first generation of elders afraid of their children. Drug dealers hold the community hostage.

Gang research showed that young males without fathers would join gangs, but eventually they would grow up and grow out of gangs and secure a job and begin to develop a family. Life in gangs has now become indefinite because of drugs. Gangs have become almost like a pharmaceutical sales force. Young boys are recruited in gangs as early as six years of age and many of them remain gang members for the rest of their life, or as long as they can continue to sell drugs.

The devastation of drugs is not just to the underclass. The drug problems cross race, income, and gender lines. That's why my pastor, Bill Winston, reminds us that Satan hates all of us, Black, White, male, female across income strata. Middle-income families have been destroyed because they could not resist the lure of drugs.

In my work with school districts worldwide, I've discovered that drug profits definitely compete against academic achievement. In what other industry can an illiterate, high school drop out earn $20,000 a day? Many young African American males will walk up to a working adult, especially their teachers, and ask, "How much money do you make in a year?" After they hear the answer, they say, "I make that in a day."

How do we protect and safeguard our children when older drug users give our young boys gym shoes, starter jackets, and jewelry? How do struggling single parent mothers convince their sons to resist that temptation? Will Nancy Reagan's phrase, "just say no," be enough?

The war on drugs was stepped up with the unfortunate death of the famous basketball player from the University of Maryland and number one draft choice for the Boston Celtics in the late '80s, Len Bias. As a result of the overdose by this brilliant athlete who never got a chance to play in the NBA, and because it cost the Boston Celtics a large amount of money, legislators overreacted. In 1986 they created the Anti-Drug Abuse and the Violent Crime Act, mandatory sentencing, and the disparity of 100:1 ratio between cocaine and crack. Crack possession receives 100 times greater punishment than cocaine possession.

Help me understand how 499 grams of cocaine receives a slap on the wrist and a homework assignment while five grams of its derivative, crack cocaine, receives a five year mandatory sentence? Judges hate this legislation and have gone on record expressing their displeasure.

Congressional leaders Maxine Waters, John Conyers, and numerous others have tried their best to change the legislation, but even that does not get to the root problem. They are considering reducing the ratio from 100:1 to 50:1 and possibly 10:1; but the major question is why does the disparity exist between cocaine and crack? Is it because cocaine is more expensive? Is it because crack is cheaper? Is it because White middle-income users primarily use cocaine? Is it because low-income people, primarily people of color, and specifically African American males, use crack? Why is there a need to take away a judge's discretion? Isn't their job to issue the appropriate sentence for the appropriate crime? With mandatory sentencing we don't need judges; secretaries could administer that.

Help me to understand how Whites are 77 percent of marijuana users, 73 percent of cocaine users, 66 percent of crack users but only 26 percent of those sentenced for drug use. How do we reconcile that African Americans are 13 percent of drug users, but 35 percent of those arrested for drug possession, 55 percent of those convicted, and 74 percent of those sentenced? [47] If there is a war on drugs, shouldn't the figures be reversed? Is there a war on drug users or a war on African American males?

This is a state of emergency. What slavery did not do to the Black family is being finished off with crack cocaine. Seventy percent of the 6,500 homicides committed in Black America are because of drugs. Sixty percent of all inmates in federal prisons and 30 percent of inmates in state prisons are there because of drugs. [48] We must contact our government officials and join Families Against Mandatory Minimums because this has reached epidemic proportions. We are clearly in a state of emergency. Forty-four percent of all drug arrests are young people under 21 years of age. In the following chapter on prisons, we will discuss that in more detail.

When I speak to young people I ask them, "Will you make more money as a drug dealer or as a school-teacher?" They laugh and almost all of them choose drug dealer. I then show them that in three separate studies drug dealers were found to average $700 a month or $8,400 per year. If they last ten years this is equivalent to $84,000.

Teacher salaries average $30,000 per year or almost $21,000 more than drug dealers. Our youth only remember their best day where they made thousands. I ask them if they know one dealer who has sold drugs for 30 years, retired, and is today living off a pension? I then teach them that drug dealers don't retire. They use, die, or go to jail.

Unfortunately, many young people believe the above will not happen to them. I understand. They also think they'll be one of the seven in a million who will join the NBA. That's why young people need adults who will give them a sense of direction. We are in a state of emergency and every adult needs to talk to a young African American male and convince him that the odds are still better in education and legal employment than selling drugs.

As an African American leader and scholar for the past three decades, I know the challenges of trying to empower the Black community and overcome the obstacles of racism, sexism, classism, monopoly capitalism, poor health care, a school system that miseducates our children, and a community that lacks self-love and Africentricity. If that was not enough, we now have to address the drug problem, an overzealous police force, and unfair legislation.

Romans 4:17 says, "Call those things that do not exist as if they are." Can you imagine a Black community as drug free? We need to begin to visualize that. My friend James Meeks, pastor of Salem Baptist Church in Chicago and Vice President of Operation Push, had this vision for his community. Do you know how hard it is to remove liquor stores from the Black community? His church and community won! We need drug free, crack free communities.

If drugs were not enough of an obstacle in the Black community, my friend Reverend Al Sharpton says that DWB (driving while Black) may be the greatest challenge to the African American community. Why should we have to plan extra time to get to a destination just in case we get pulled over by police? Many African Americans even reroute their trip because their experience has taught them that there is a much greater chance they will be pulled over in certain neighborhoods.

Research has shown that 70 percent of Whites believe racism is not a significant problem in America while almost the same percentage of African Americans believe it is the major problem in America. [49] Many Whites believe the police department serves and protects even when they saw Rodney King being beat 39 times. In a court of law they felt that he was resisting arrest.

Just as Clarence Thomas negated 50 million people who voted for Gore, he did the same in the 1996 case of Whren vs. the United States Supreme Court. The question before the court was, are car searches constitutional? In its friend of the court brief the ACLU argued that the pretexual searches violate the core principals of the Fourth Amendment and warned that to sanction such searches was to invite discriminatory enforcement. The court did not heed their warning, however; and instead declared that any traffic offense committed by a driver was a legitimate basis for a stop regardless of the officer's subjective state of mind. Clarence Thomas voted in favor of giving police officers the right to search any car they choose. In practice their indecision has given the police virtually unlimited authority to stop and search any vehicle they want. In April 2001 this was exacerbated with Clarence and his colleagues with the Atwater vs. U.S. Supreme Court. Police can stop and arrest people with such minor infractions as not wearing a seat belt. Driving While Black will become more dangerous under this police state.

Every driver probably violates some provision of the vehicle code at some time even during a short drive because the traffic code identifies so many different infractions. For example, traffic codes define precisely how long a driver must signal before turning and the particular conditions on which a driver must use lights. Vehicle equipment is also highly regulated. A small light bulb must illuminate the rear license plate. Tail lights must be visible from a particular distance, tire tread must be at a particular depth, and all equipment must be in working order at all times. If police targets a driver for stop and search, all they have to do is come up with a pretext for a stop and then follow the car until the driver makes an inconsequential error or until a technical violation is observed.

The story of Robert Gardner is typical. Gardner was stopped while driving a Lexus on I-95. A laboratory technician at North Bronx Hospital in New York, Gardner was driving with his cousin to visit family in South Carolina when he was pulled over for speeding. The officer asked him to sit in the patrol car and peppered him with questions. Where are you going? What is your job? When are you going back? Then the officer went to Gardner's car and asked the same questions of his cousin, Sharon. He then got permission from Gardner to search his car. "I thought he was just going to look in my glove compartment and trunk," but he said the officer opened the alarm system and compact disc player. He removed door panels, molding and seats. He let air out of the tires and knocked on them. Then he deflated the spare tire and bounced it on the road. He found nothing. Gardner told the newspaper that he left the scene with a $25 seatbelt ticket and annoying vibration in his Lexus and the belief that he had been treated unfairly. "He claimed I was speeding but never gave me a ticket."

How do we explain African Americans who are less than 20 percent of the population in most states being the victims of DWB more than 50 percent of the time in numerous states? The ACLU has filed lawsuits challenging the police practice of racial profiling in eight states. The statistical evidence collected in the course of this litigation shows a clear pattern of racial and discriminatory traffic stops and searches.

Congresspersons John Conyers, Stephanie Jones, and Eleanor Holmes have introduced legislation called the Racial Profiling Prohibition Act that requires the collection of several categories of data on each traffic stop, including the race of the driver and whether a search was performed. North Carolina has become the first state to pass legislation to help quantify the DWB. Every city and state needs to pass legislation that will quantify the extent of this national problem. In addition, the justice department needs to also monitor the extent of this problem and deny states funding for highways if discrimination exists.

In the meantime, African American parents need to teach their sons how to handle a police encounter. Numerous rites of passage programs, mentoring programs, and families have developed role-playing strategies to teach males how to handle this state of emergency. How unfortunate that we now must teach African American males that some police officers are not there to serve and protect them. The Congressional Black Caucus Task Force on Law Enforcement Misconduct, responding to community concerns about police misconduct, held hearings during 1999 in Washington, D.C., New York, Chicago, and Los Angeles. The general text utilizes many of the questions asked by participants in these hearings. The following are examples of situations that occur fairly frequently in some communities:

You are walking down the street and the police stop you to ask you some routine questions. Do you have to answer?

NO. Even if you are in an area designated for a "high crime area" it is well within your constitutional rights not be answer, in fact you may leave. If the officer continues to bother you, get the officer's name and badge number. File a complaint with the appropriate agency in your community.

You live in a neighborhood that is known for drug dealing, and police come to your home without a search warrant to search for an original Jacob Lawrence painting stolen from the Smithsonian. Must you allow them to search your house?

NO. They must have a valid search warrant in hand.

You are a high school student. The principal suspects that you have a weapon in your bag and asks if she can search it. You respond, "No, I have a Fourth Amendment right against unreasonable search." The principal then grabs your bag and searches and finds a water gun. Was the search of your bag legal?

YES. The search of students' lockers and bags by school authorities has been routinely upheld as legal as long as the school officials have reasonable suspicion that it contains anything that violates school rules.

The police stop you for doing 45 mph in a 30 mph zone. Upon approaching your car the officer has his band on his holster, he requests you to get out of the car, and he proceeds to do a pat down of your person. Is this legal?

YES and NO. The Supreme Court has ruled that an officer can request you to get out of the car. The officer cannot pat you down, however, unless the officer has a reasonable suspicion that you are armed.

You and your friends are having a "Sweet 16" birthday party at your house. A neighbor calls the police to complain of loud music. The police arrive and request to come in. Must you allow them in?

NO. They must have a warrant to gain entry. The complaint of loud music is insufficient reason to serve as an exception to Fourth Amendment protection. They can request you turn the music down so as not to disturb the neighbors.

You allow the police to come into your home when they arrive to investigate a neighbor's complaint of loud music. They smell marijuana. The police begin searching your home. Is the search valid?

No. The odor of marijuana gives the police probable cause to believe marijuana is in your home. However, they cannot conduct a search of your home without a warrant or a valid exception to the warrant requirement, such as your consenting to the search.

You are in a "high crime" area and you are aware that the police have a history of harassing kids in the neighborhood. When you see the police you automatically run. Can the police stop and search you given the fact that you saw them and ran?

YES. The Supreme Court has held that flight alone in a high crime area creates sufficient reasonable suspicion for police to stop and search you.

You are an African American male driving a Lexus in a predominately White community and the police pull you over. When asked why you were stopped the officer said your car looked unfamiliar and he thought you might be lost. Is the stop legal?

NO. This is a classic example of racial profiling.

You are a passenger in a car that has just been stopped by police for a faulty brake light. The officer notices that the driver has a hypodermic syringe in his shirt pocket and the driver admits that he uses it for drugs. The officer begins to search the car for illegal drugs. Your briefcase is on the back seat. The officer opens your (the passenger's) briefcase without your permission and finds illegal drugs. Is the search of your briefcase without your permission legal?

YES. The Supreme Court has ruled that a police officer with probable cause to search a car may search a passenger's belongings found in the car that are capable of concealing the items for which the officer is searching.

You are standing on a street corner with two of your best friends. The police approach you based on an anonymous tip that you are carrying a gun. They conduct a frisk and search of your person without your consent and find a gun. Was the frisk and search of your person legal?

NO. The Supreme Court has ruled that law enforcement officers may not stop and frisk individuals merely based on an anonymous tip.

You are a resident of a public housing complex and the police are conducting a search of all the units for drugs and weapons. Must you allow them to search your unit?

NO. The police cannot search your unit unless they have a valid search warrant or an exception to the warrant requirement, such as your consent.
The police are doing a sweep of your unit only. Must you allow them to go in?

NO. You can refuse to allow a search or your apartment unless they have a valid search warrant.

You were arrested at your place of employment on charges unrelated to drug-delivery. Several months go by and police believe that your car may have been used to deliver drugs. You are in a state that requires instruments used for criminality to be seized. However, your car is parked in a public place. The police tow your car to the station and conduct an inventory search. During the search they find drugs in your ashtray and charge you with possession of controlled substance. Was the seizure of your car legal? Was the subsequent search or your vehicle legal?

YES and YES. The Supreme Court ruled that in this situation officers have probable cause to believe the vehicle could be seized. The seizure of the car in a public place does not violate the Fourth Amendment. Also, the inventory search was a legal search.

You are staying at a hotel and are out visiting a friend. The police ask the manager of the hotel if they can search your room. The manager opens the door for the police and they begin a search of your room? Is the search legal?

NO. They must have a valid search warrant. The manager does not have the authority to consent to a search of your room. A hotel guest is given the same constitutional protections as in their home.

You are a student and you live in the dormitory. The police suspect that you have gold in your room from a bank robbery. You happen to be away from your room, so the police ask the dorm director to open your door, and the dorm director does. The police conduct a search and find the gold from the bank heist. Is the search of your room valid?

NO. Whether you are in a private or state-run school, in order for the search to be valid police must have a search warrant or an exception to the warrant requirement. The dorm is your home and the dorm director cannot consent for you.

You have been drinking and there is no question that you are intoxicated. Somehow you manage to drive home. The police receive a tip from a reliable source that you were swerving on the highway. Approximately five minutes after you walk into your house, the police arrive. The police ask through the door had you just been driving and you respond in a slurred voice "yes." The police ask to come in, and you respond "no!" The police, in an effort to preserve evidence of your drunk driving, force their way in and announce that you are under arrest for Driving Under the Influence (DUI) of alcohol. Is this seizure valid?

NO. They must get a warrant to arrest you in your own house, especially if the arrest is for a minor offense.

The police have forced their way into your home to preserve evidence for the charge of DUI. While they are in your home they see a radio, which they suspect is stolen. One of the officers moves the radio to get the serial number. He finds jewelry that is on the most recent stolen goods list. Can the officer seize the jewelry and use it against you at trial?

NO. The police were not lawfully inside your home. Even if they had been lawfully inside either because you consented to them entering or they had a warrant for your arrest for drunken driving, the radio would be outside the scope of your consent or the arrest warrant and the jewelry was not in plain view. Moving the radio was a search. For this search to be lawful, the officers would have to possess probable cause to believe the radio was stolen and have either a warrant or a valid exception to the Fourth Amendment to move it. A hunch or suspicion is not enough.

The Drug Industry

The police have followed you to your house and they look through the blinds, which are open and see you and two other men placing a powdery substance that appears to be cocaine in plastic bags. The officers kick the door in and arrest all three of you. Is the arrest valid and can the drugs be used against you at trial?

YES and NO. The officers' actions were based on the "plain view" doctrine. The Supreme Court has held, however, that the police must knock and announce themselves before kicking in the door. Since often this is done in quick succession, assuming they did so, the arrest is valid and the prosecutors can use the evidence seized against you at trial.

The police approach you and say you fit the description of an alleged rapist. The police say in order to clear this up and eliminate you as a potential suspect they want to get a sample of your DNA. Must you submit to the DNA request?

NO. The police must have a warrant or your consent.

You threw away a plan to embezzle a million dollars from Bank of America. Nonetheless, you follow through with the plan exactly as written. The police receive a tip from a source that you embezzled the money. The police secure a search warrant for your house. A search of the house comes up empty. The police decide to search your garbage can, which is located inside the garage attached to your house. You object to the search of your garbage can. While searching the garbage can the officers find the plan and place you under arrest. Was the search of the garbage can without a warrant or consent legal?

NO. The warrant was for the house only and did not mention the garage oar the garbage can. Although, generally anything in a garbage can outside your home is considered abandoned and not protected by the Fourth Amendment, since this garbage can had not been "set out" an expectation of privacy would probably still attach to it. If the can had been place at the curb, outside what is considered the boundary of your home (curtilage) it would not be protected by the Fourth Amendment.

You are at the airport. According to the airport police, you fit the profile of someone carrying drugs (drug courier). The officer notices a bulge in your pockets and has a hunch that it is drugs. Can the officer detain you under the theory of reasonable suspicion?

NO. To detain you under the theory of reasonable suspicion the officer must possess more than a hunch. There must be specific facts that lead to the suspicion.

The State Police stop you for a broken taillight. The officer discovers that your license has been suspended and places you under arrest. After placing you in the police cruiser the officer begins to search your car. Specifically, he looks in the glove compartment and finds a container. He opens the container and finds counterfeit money. Is the search of the glove compartment valid? What about the search of the container? What about the search of the trunk?

YES, YES and NO. After you have been arrested the officer can search the glove compartment of the car and containers found therein. This is the doctrine known as search incident to arrest. The officer cannot search the trunk of the car at this time without probable cause to believe there is something in the trunk. It is not sufficient that counterfeit money was found in the glove compartment.

The State police arrest you for driving while drunk and leaving the scene of an accident and take you into custody. They tow your car to the police parking lot. Once on the lot, they search the car and find marijuana in the trunk. Is this search legal?

Yes. This is called an "inventory search." Once the police have lawfully taken a vehicle into custody this type of search is permitted to protect the owner's property while in custody; protect the police against claims of lost or stolen property; and, protect the police from potential danger.

You are employed by a private hospital as a nurses' aide. The hospital does random drug testing. You tested positive for cocaine and were fired. Did the hospital violate your right to be secure in your person guaranteed by the Fourth Amendment?

NO. Drug tests have been held not to violate the Fourth Amendment. Moreover, the Fourth Amendment only protects you against invasions of your privacy by government officials or those acting as agents of the government.

You have just arrived in New York from a trip to Jamaica. You have gotten your bags and the airport police and police dog come up to you and dog sniffs your luggage. The airport police ask you to step into a room and hold you for 2 hours, checking your identification and asking you questions about your trip. Is the dog sniff a violation of the Fourth Amendment? Is the 2-hour detention by the police a violation of the Fourth Amendment?

NO and YES. The airport police can subject your luggage to a dog sniff without having a reasonable suspicion. However, they cannot detain you without a reasonable suspicion and the detention cannot be for an unreasonable length of time. The Supreme Court has held that a detention of 90 minutes based only on a reasonable suspicion was unreasonable and, therefore, violated the Fourth Amendment.

In *Countering the Conspiracy to Destroy Black Boys*, I wrote that males must know the distinction between a *battle* and a *war*. Our males need to understand that when they are pulled over by police this is not the time to be macho. We must teach our African American males that it is better to lose the battle, be inconvenienced, and embarrassed by the police but be available for the war which includes marrying the mother of your children, being gainful employed, making a difference in your community, and testifying later to put the police officer behind bars.

How rampant is police abuse in the African American community? In the early 1990s the U.S. Justice Department began an investigation into the systemic abuse perpetrated by a number of White police officers in the 39th police district of Philadelphia. Evidence showed that these officers were planting drugs on African Americans, assaulting them during arrest, and wrongfully obtaining their prosecution and conviction. Ultimately, six officers were tried, convicted, and incarcerated for their criminal activities.

The Drug Industry

The Ramparts Police District in Los Angeles had a drug team called Crash Community Resources Against the Street. The police stole drugs, murdered innocent people, and falsified evidence. Fortunately, one of the police officers was caught stealing a pound of cocaine worth $1 million. He squealed to protect himself and this started the investigation, which led to 20 officers being fired, 30 convicted, and 70 are under investigation. More than 100 defendants were dismissed and 1,000 are being investigated.[50] Some Whites ask, "Could this happen in America? Could our police department do that?"

Everyone should read Gary Webb's book *Dark Alliance* and his web page. In the book he details the relationship between the Contras, Nicaragua, CIA, FBI, and the infusion of drugs into South Central Los Angeles. Government agencies injected cheap cocaine into South Central Los Angeles. They used the Bloods and Crips as distribution agents. The major players were Contra leaders Danilo Blandon, and Norwin Meneses, CIA agent Enrique Benmudez, and gang leader Ricky Ross. Ricky was so successful distributing crack in Los Angeles that he coordinated its distribution nationwide. Why was Gary Webb fired from the *San Jose Mercury*? Why was he denounced by the larger media? Why is it that we still do not believe that there could be some conspiratorial thread between Tulsa, Tuskegee, Centreville, Mississippi, and South Central Los Angeles?

Have our police departments become contaminated? Have they been infected by drug money? Each year law enforcement is given $1 trillion by the government to fight drugs. They also receive $3 billion via asset forfeiture. Many police departments are actually financing their budgets off assets secured from drug raids. If that was not enough, some police officers take money as they shake down drug users.

When reporters interview police officials about the progress of the war on drugs, many officers say, "We can't win yet because we still have too many bills to be paid." This is an industry that feeds off itself. Crime does pay for the people who administrate the system. Out of control, this industry, for the past three decades, has spent $30 trillion. If the war on drugs ended, there would be a recession in this country. Could the country absorb a trillion dollar annual loss?

Could police departments function without the $3 billion in asset forfeiture? How successful have the drug wars been? In 1981, the DEA secured 4,263 pounds of cocaine. In the year 2000 they secured 300,000 kilos of cocaine. I guess you could say they've been successful by securing more cocaine; but is that really a success or does it merely show how demand and supply have increased?

The coastguard has only been able to intercede and prevent 10 percent of all drugs into America. In 1980, the DEA reported 581,000 arrests for drug possession. In 2000, it was two million. [51] Few kingpins are prosecuted. Out of 57 convictions in the Eastern District of Missouri, 55 of the defendants were Black, one was White, one was Hispanic, and not one kingpin was among them. Three of the 56 defendants were jointly charged with having 944 grams, three others had 454 grams among them, and one had 451 grams. The other 50 had a total of less than 2000 grams, averaging less than 40 grams each. Eight defendants had less than 10 grams. Five of them had less than a gram, barely enough to detect or to utilize. The total amount of crack cocaine for 56 of the 57 defendants (the amount for one defendant was not determined) was less than 4,000 grams. Powder cocaine is usually imported into this country by boats, trucks, and planes, and in huge quantities. Kingpin dealers are then able to transport the drug in brick-like packages referred to as "kilos." A kilogram weighs 1,000 grams. Thus, it appears clear that the removal of this small quantity of drugs would hardly reduce the supply of crack cocaine.

It appears that the war on drug has been successful, but is that true? How many people in possession of drugs were not arrested? Does this simply illustrate the massive extent of drug use in America? Of those arrested only 11 percent were major dealers and 89 percent were street hustlers. Every arrest in America costs $150,000. If an individual receives the unfortunate mandatory minimum of five years at $30,000 per shot, that's an additional $150,000. [52] That's $300,000 we are spending for every drug arrest!

The Partnership for a Drug Free America is also a program that is out of control. Corporations such as Disney and other media giants receive money to develop ads to discourage drug use. What a joke! These ads are not as effective as community-based prevention, intervention, and treatment programs. Two billion dollars have been allocated to media giants when the DEA's research clearly illustrates that the money could have been used to purchase every single cocoa leaf grown in South America for one year. [53]

In the book *Fight Back*, Michael Levin documents the absurdity of America's drug policy. There is an equation that shows that enforcing criminal laws against dealers has about as much of a chance of impacting the drug problem as your Honda Civic has of breaking the sound barrier. Here is the equation: Number of potential drug dealers, plus world demand, divided by the number of narcotics officers and available budget, equals total absurdity of the U.S. drug war policy. The war on drugs is not working.

However, the war on African American males has been successful. Sixty percent of inmates are there because of drugs. This is a state of emergency. As a result, we have to look at extreme measures. Should we decriminalize drugs? Should we legalize drugs? What effect would that have on the African American community? If drugs were legal, 60 percent of the 1.3 million African American males in jail would be free. Seventy percent of African Americans who are victims of homicide would be alive because they would not have fought over drug turf. Gangs would be less significant in the African American community. There would be fewer gangs and our boys would stay in them a shorter period of time because there would be no financial incentive to stay longer.

If drugs were decriminalized or legalized then the profit motive would be eliminated and our youth would have to pursue education as an economic alternative. African Americans would no longer fear losing their possessions. Elders, women, and children would feel safe walking through the community. Thousands of African American males who have been disenfranchised would regain their rights and the Florida debacle would not have happened.

The DEA is not in favor of decriminalizing or legalizing drugs, but do they have an objective opinion? Do they have a vested interest in the maintenance of the war on drugs? If drugs were decriminalized or legalized, these guys would lose their job. They would lose $1 trillion annually. They would not receive $3 billion in asset forfeitures. Many prisons would close and the annual $20 billion would be reduced by 60 percent.

What have other countries done about their drug problem? Europe is an excellent place to analyze the effect of decriminalization. Before Russia implemented decriminalization they had 110,000 hard-core drug addicts. That number has now risen to 7 million. In 1960, Britain began prescribing heroin. Four decades later the addiction of heroin has increased by 30 percent. A similar increase in addiction has occurred in the Netherlands and Switzerland. The DEA is quick to remind us about Zurich's Needle Park and how it became a tremendous liability to the country. What the media and DEA forgot to tell us was that 70 percent of the people in Needle Park were foreigners. They had traveled to Zurich because their country had not decriminalized drugs.

In addition to decriminalization and legalization, let's also add, "harm reduction." In America, a drug addict tends to be unemployed and has a criminal record. Sixty percent are HIV infected. [54] In Europe a drug addict is employed, a taxpayer, and only one percent is infected. How could this be? They both are drug users.

Under decriminalization, harm reduction provides for so-called "tolerance zones." In other words, drug use in designated areas is tolerated. In these tolerance zones, there are injection rooms, in which medical staff provides clean needles and counseling. Users also receive condoms. There's nothing like it in America. All drug use here is done in the dark and in secret, in alleyways, in crack houses, and behind the closed doors of suburban homes and very expensive hotel rooms.

Imagine what it would be like if the American government decided to decriminalize or legalize cocaine and heroin. Not only would addiction rates increase, public health and safety would be put in serious jeopardy. How could we survive with drug using pilots, surgeons, and other significant health and safety professionals? What would be the state of our product safety? Can we fathom the exponential increase in car accidents? The former mayor of Baltimore, Kurt Schmoke, says, "We will allow you to use them but it doesn't negate corporations denying you the opportunity to work." Decriminalizing or legalizing drugs would simply increase mandatory drug testing before you could fly an airplane or perform surgery. Still, how would we monitor every driver?

At a global conference in London, 112 countries rejected the idea of legalizing drugs. Ninety percent of youth do not use drugs in America because they are illegal. [55] Because the DEA and the larger White society would be affected financially, proposals to decriminalize and legalize drugs have not passed. I do think we should look at the success Europe has had with harm reduction. AIDS is now the number one killer of young African American males. Homicide is a leading killer for African American male teenagers. With the harm reduction approach, there is less chance of drug users becoming HIV infected. America should consider tolerance zones and injection rooms. Harm reduction would force America to reallocate drug expenditures toward better treatment, prevention, and intervention. Presently two-thirds of drug funds are allocated toward enforcement and only one-sixth to treatment.

The Rand Corporation reports that treatment is 15 times more cost-effective than mandatory sentencing. One dollar spent in treatment saves $4 to $7 in crime and prison costs. [56] Kurt Schmoke has said for years, "The drug problem is not going to be solved by the Attorney General, but by the Surgeon General. Jails don't stop drugs just as cemeteries don't stop death."

The Drug Industry

The American Medical Association believes that drug addiction is a disease, not a criminal offense. Sixty percent of inmates are in jail because of drug-related crimes, yet only nine percent receive treatment. African Americans are 70 percent of those arrested for drugs, but Whites are 66 percent of those receiving drug treatment.

How effective has drug treatment been? In three separate studies in California, Texas, and Delaware only 26 percent of 282 drug users returned to jail in the state of Texas. [57] In California only 27 percent of 162 drug users returned to jail after receiving treatment. In Delaware only 31 percent of 300 drug users returned to jail. In the following chapter on prisons, we will talk about the U.S. 85 percent recidivism rate. Methadone treatment costs the American taxpayer $4,700, compared to jail time, which costs between $18,000 and $38,000.

An excellent program is Drug Court. It was founded in 1989 because of the tremendous backlog on the American judicial system. Drug court is not available to drug dealers or if the accused was involved in a violent act. There are now 500 courts nationwide. Not only have they reduced the backlog, they help drug users overcome their addiction without incarceration. Mandatory drug tests on a regular basis are required. If you are not present for drug court, you automatically are sentenced. Drug courts provide treatment and counseling.

Since 1989, 100,000 drug users have gone through drug court with a completion record of 71 percent. It only costs the American taxpayer $2,500 per offender. [58] This boggles my mind. Why would America spend $18,000 to $38,000 per year to incarcerate an inmate and $30 trillion on drug enforcement when harm reduction, drug treatment, and drug courts have a success rate that hovers near 70 percent?

While African Americans are only 13 percent of drug users, they are 35 percent of those arrested, 55 percent of those convicted, and 74 percent of those sentenced. Why is the number increasing in the African American population? Why are we not 13 percent of those arrested? Why is there a disparity between the 35 percent that are arrested and the 74 percent that are sentenced? Why are more Whites being placed in drug courts and more African Americans being placed in prisons? Every effort should be made by legislators and community activists to increase the number of African Americans placed in drug treatment programs and drug courts.

We're in a state of emergency, and just as we need a moratorium on African American males being placed in special education, we need a moratorium on African American males being placed in jail for drug use. Drug court and treatment should be the first option, not jail. In fact, all African American males and females who are incarcerated because of drug use should be transferred to drug court.

We can learn from Europe, but an even better answer may lie in Asia. At the end of World War II, China had a staggering 70 million heroin and opium addicts. When Mao's army conquered Mainland China in 1949, the priority was to suppress drug addiction, not to war against drug dealers. You may believe that China's success was due to executions. Only twenty-seven Chinese were executed out of *70 million* heroin and opium addicts. China implemented a national policy of mandatory treatment and incarceration. The program was accompanied by anti-drug propaganda. Although drug users were depicted as the "enemy," redemption through rehabilitation was possible and encouraged. In other words, China intended to save and redeem the addicts whether they liked it or not. By the spring of 1951, less than two years after the program's inception, China's drug problem was eradicated. [59]

Japan's drug problem was at its height in 1963 when that country decided to follow China's lead and passed a law that committed drug users to mental hospitals. A propaganda campaign vilified drug users as the destroyers of a safe, sane society. It became the duty of each community to identify drug users. In less than three years the Japanese were as successful as the Chinese. [60]

Do you think the DEA is not aware of the success of Japan, China, and Europe? Why is it the DEA loves to talk about some isolated failures in Europe rather than the successes experienced in countries around the world?

There are two kinds of treatment: treatment on demand and mandatory treatment. Virtually all funding goes toward treatment on demand. The assumption is that heavy drug users want to be treated. Unfortunately, this assumption goes against the weight of evidence. Despite the increase of treatment on demand programs, the number of hard-core addicts, approximately 15 million, has remained constant over the past decade. We are not winning the war on drugs. The only way to win this war is to go after the buyer, not the seller.

Remember, more than 70 percent of drug users in America are White. The focus of the war on drugs should be on this population, not small-time Black drug dealers. Moreover, the success of drug court is not due to voluntary testing and treatment. Those users clearly understand that if they do not submit themselves to a drug test and treatment, the consequence is jail.

Surely the DEA is aware of Michael Levine's research and program, "Fight Back." Why have they not implemented it? I strongly endorse the program. Drugs are a business, and the American way of business is all about supply and demand. Supply follows demand, not vice versa. If no one bought drugs, dealers would go out of business.

When the media needs a story, the DEA will provide them with a drug bust so that Americans will feel their $1 trillion is being used successfully. Yet, whenever the police make a drug bust, the dealers are back out on the street or replacements have already taken over their turf within hours. Imagine how frustrating it must be for sincere police officers, having spent days, weeks, and months on a case, to know that the bad guys probably will not spend much time in jail. And for the community, which calls the police time and again, only to bump into the drug dealers on the street the next day. The police pick up one dealer, and another is there to continue the activity.

The best way to solve the drug problem is by taking the same approach communities used to stop prostitution. If you eliminate the demand, there will be no need for the supply, so these communities went after the John. Police made his seedy habit more trouble than it was worth. His picture was placed on the front page of the newspaper and on television. The problem was shared with his employer and wife. He had to do community service at women's shelters. His driver's license was taken away. As a result, John had a different view on prostitution. And, compared to the amount of money we spend to incarcerate inmates, these strategies cost very little money.

Our drug war is all wrong. We are looking at supply side economics. That is not the way to address the industry.

We must go after drug users. Users do not like to be inconvenienced. In general, users have families, own homes, are employees and taxpayers—they just want to avoid reality and get high.

Do you think the DEA is not aware that they are going after the wrong person? With the amount of intelligence in the DEA, shouldn't they know that they would be more effective if they went after the users?

Would sellers have a market if there were no users? If the DEA went after users and made their lives inconvenient, do you think the sellers would still be on the corner? If we made drug users receive mandatory treatment, allocated more money for drug court, and provided harm reduction centers for drug users, would that not solve the drug problem in America? If police departments worked with community organizations to monitor drug users and post signs all over the community, take pictures and video tape drug sales, do you think that would solve the drug problem in America? We are in a state of emergency, and Fight Back, drug court, harm reduction centers, mandatory treatment, and the legalization of marijuana are all needed to resolve the problem.

In closing, America does not have a drug problem. America has a moral problem. We struggle not against flesh and blood, but against principalities and rulers in high places. America only has six percent of the world's population, but consumes more than 60 percent of the drugs. America reminds me of Rome, Sodom, and Gomorrah, and unfortunately, African Americans have begun to act like the Romans. God has given us free will. You can choose crack or Christ, liquor or the Lord, heroin or the Holy Spirit, but you will choose. God created us all with a significant void in our lives, and then he gave us free will. Unfortunately, many of us have chosen Satan over Christ. Satan has led us to believe that he will give us joy. One of his greatest tricks has been drugs, and they are destroying America and specifically African American males.

While self-help groups (e.g., Alcoholics Anonymous), harm reduction centers, mandatory treatment programs, drug court, and Fight Back are excellent strategies, they do not get to the root of the problem.

I Corinthians 6:19–20 addresses the problem:

"Do you not know that your body is the temple of the Holy Spirit, who is in you, whom you have from God? You are not your own, for you were bought at a price. Therefore glorify God in your body and in your spirit which are God's."

In addition, Romans 12:1–2 says:

"I beseech you therefore my brethren by the mercies of God that you present your bodies a living sacrifice holy acceptable to God which is your reasonable service. Do not be conformed to this world but be transformed by the renewing of your mind that you may prove what is that good and acceptable and perfect will of God."

The Bible also reminds us in II Corinthians 10:4:

"For the weapons of our warfare are not carnal but mighty in God for the pulling down of strongholds."

The Drug Industry

Drugs are spirits. They are strongholds, thus the weapons of our warfare must ultimately go beyond harm reduction centers, treatment programs, Fight Back, and drug court. While these can be viable solutions and alleviate our drug problem, we need the help of the Holy Spirit. We need to bind the demon of drug use. Matthew 18:18 says, "Whatever you bind on earth will be bound in heaven, whatever you loose on earth will be loosed in heaven."

I recommend that self-help groups and treatment programs be Christian-based. Numerous users have told me that they felt strong when they were in the Alcoholics Anonymous, Cocaine Anonymous, and Heroin Anonymous meetings, but when they were not around their peer group and counselors, they became weak. Former users must be strong whether alone or by themselves. Lasting strength only comes from constant fellowship with the Lord Jesus Christ. Until drug users get saved, the penal population will continue to grow. In the following chapter, we will look at the penal industry that is destroying African American males, their families, and their communities.

STATE

OF

EMERGENCY

5

THE PENAL SYSTEM

American Whites have divided the world into two major categories: the First World and Third World. America is the First World while countries populated by people of color comprise the Third World. What makes America first? Income? Gross national product? Investments? Savings? Research and development? While all of that is true, America also leads the world in divorce, suicide, homicide, gun ownership, incarceration rates, drug use, and income disparity. In America, one percent of the population owns 48 percent of the wealth; ten percent owns 86 percent of the wealth.

How does it feel, living in the richest country in the world, earning less than $10,000, while watching people on television live lavishly? What is it like for African American males, living in housing projects, while watching videos of people living in mansions? Let me put this into a quantitative context with the following chart:

Country	Incarceration rate per 100,000
United States	730
Russian	690
Ukraine	390

South Africa	265
Canada	115
China	103
England	100
France	95
Germany	85
Greece	55
Japan	37
India	24 [61]

For every 100,000 Americans, 730 are incarcerated, and this only includes federal and state prisons. It does not include local jails and people under probation. Furthermore, when you dissect the 730, for every 100,000 White males in America, 461 Whites will be incarcerated, but for every 100,000 African American males, the figure leaps to 3,250. The 730 figure reflects the total population, which also includes women. Even more significant is that for every 100,000 African American males in America, 3,250 are incarcerated (and remember that does not include local jails and probation).

The Penal System

Let me put this within a larger context. In 1993, the last of year of apartheid in South Africa, there were 581 Black inmates per 100,000. In America, we have almost four times that number, and supposedly we are not living under apartheid. This is a state of emergency.

Could there be a correlation between economic power and a country's incarceration rate? Over the past decade, Russia's incarceration rate was greater than America's. However, within the past two years, America has exceeded Russia. On the other hand, most European countries, such as England, France, and Greece, have reduced their inmate populations. These are not poor countries, but it is obvious they are doing something different than the United States as indicated in the homicide rates listed in the following chart:

Country	Homicide Rates in Industrialized Nations per 100,000
United States	7.4
Canada	2.1
France	2.0
England	1.3
Japan	1.0 [62]

In the year 2000, 13,673 Americans were victims of homicide compared to Japan, where there were only 32 murders. What is driving this disparity between America and other countries? Why is there such a wide gap between America's and Japan's murder and incarceration rates? America can definitely learn from Japan. For example, the disparity between the haves and the have nots continues to grow in America. As a result, America is a hostile and violent society. Also, European and Japanese countries possess, for the most part, homogeneous populations and thus have a much higher regard for its citizens.

I said at the outset of this book that we do not struggle against flesh and blood, but against principalities and rulers in high places. There is an evil spirit in America. The country was founded on violence. America was taken from the Native Americans. Africans were brought to America as slaves and forced to work for 246 years. One percent of the population makes critical decisions that have very little regard for the poor. One-third of all adult inmates in the world reside in the United States. How can that be? How can six percent of the world's population constitute 33 percent of all inmates?

Is there a relationship between slavery and the American penal system? A careful analysis of the 13th Amendment illustrates that inmates forfeit all rights to freedom. States can make them work for free, place them on chain gangs and keep them in "the hole" indefinitely, etc. Could America have been the richest country in the world without free labor building its economic foundation between 1619 and 1865? Are African American males, fodder for the penal system? How significant is the American penal system? Does the penal budget now compete with the military budget? Each one receives almost one-third of the total U.S. budget. How many schools could have been built with that money? How many Americans could have received medical insurance? How many jobs could have been created if America greatly reduced its penal and military budget?

Today, prisons are big business and they are growing at about 25 percent per year. By the year 2020, the system will receive funds equivalent to the military budget.

There are five million Americans under the supervision of the penal system. [63] To put this into context, in 1982 when I released *Countering the Conspiracy to Destroy Black Boys Vol. I*, there were less than 100,000 African American males in jail; today there are more than 1.3 million. In 1980, the budget for the penal system was $7 billion. Just two decades later, it is now a 150 billion dollar industry. [64] The system may appear to be out of control, but you can believe, the ruling class knows exactly what it's doing.

The private sector has now moved into the prison business. Bonds are sold via the stock market. The best way to understand this industry is to view it like the hotel industry. Imagine the Hyatt, Hilton, or Marriott being guaranteed two million customers sleeping in their rooms every night. Each prison has to provide meals, soap, toothpaste, towels, toilet paper, linens, blankets, telephones, etc. The list goes on and on, and this is why prisons have become a big money maker for America.

Let me give you an example. Dial Soap Company secured a contract for $100,000 with just one New York City jail. Vita Pro Foods of Montreal, Canada, contracted to supply inmates in the State of Texas with its soy-based meat substitute, and the contract was worth $34 million a year. One pay telephone in a prison can generate as much as $15,000 per year.

When the State of Colorado wanted to find beds for 500 of its inmates, it called Dominion Management of Etna in Oklahoma. The company found an old mail warehouse equipped with bars in Texarkana, Texas, that could hold the prisoners (albeit 26 to a single cell with only one bathroom). The Colorado Department of Corrections agreed to pay Dominion $365,000 a year for telephone calls for as long as the inmates are in the Texas facility. [65]

Between 1980 and 1993, Presidents Ronald Reagan and George Bush, Sr. cut federal spending on employment and training by nearly 50 percent while corrections spending had increased by 521 percent. Federal, state, and local funding of the justice system literally exploded in the two decades leading up to 2000. Average direct federal, state, and local expenditures for police grew by 16 percent, court costs by 58 percent, prosecution and legal services by 152 percent, public defense by 259 percent, and corrections by 154 percent. Federal spending for justice grew by 668 percent, county spending increased by 711 percent, state spending surged by 848 percent. In California, the ratio is eight to one between inmates and college students. California allocates $31,000 to lock up a youth in a juvenile detention center, but less than $6,000 to teach elementary and high school students. [66]

The following chart illustrates a paradox: crime is declining while expenditures are increasing:

Crime	Rate Per 100,000		Percentage Change	Percentage Change in State Prisoners Between 1980 and 1995
	1980	**1995**		
All	5950	5278	-11%	+234%
Violent	597	685	+15%	+168%
Property	5353	4593	-14%	+158%
Burglary	1684	988	- 41%	+114% [67]

The Penal System

How do we reconcile the fact that spending for prisons, has increased, from $6 billion to $150 billion, while the murder rate is flat? All crime is down 11 percent, yet the number of prisoners has increased, from 500,000 in 1980 to more than two million in 2001—a 400 percent increase. Many reasons contribute to this paradox, one of which is the media. Ninety-five percent of Americans develop their perspectives based on the media. Eighty percent of Americans believe that crime is the number one problem, yet if you review the chart, you'll see that crime is actually down. [68]

Why the disconnect? Because 43 percent of local news is about violence? Because there's been a 300 percent increase in violence reporting on local news over the past decade? Could there be any correlation between the American view on crime and the fact that violent TV shows increased 74 percent over the past decade? Children have seen 40,000 murders and 200,000 acts of violence by age 18. [69]

In addition, the Reagan era launched a merger mania among media corporations. Today, nine corporations control almost 90 percent of American news. These corporations include Time-Warner, Disney, Bertelsmann, News Corporation, PCI, General Electric, Sony, Seagram, and Viacom. Within six months of acquiring BET, Viacom removed Tavis Smiley, closed their New York studio, and laid off almost 500 employees. The same holds true in the music industry. Five companies, some listed above, determine which rap CD is released, promoted, and played on the radio.

Flip the channels and it's as if you never changed the channel at all. The networks air the same news at the same time. Collusion exists among the major networks to show the same news. In addition, these major media corporations have cut their newsroom budgets for reporters even though advertising revenue has increased. Researching the facts, figures, and history behind the reduction of crime versus the increase in the prison population would be too labor intensive for these corporations' bottom line. It's easier to provide a one or two minute expose of a violent murder. It's easier to have a reporter and cameraman cover a drug deal gone bad or the aftermath of a murder than provide a five or seven minute analysis of our penal system.

Not only does the media shape our perceptions, but public policy has become very reactionary because of the media's increasingly conservative bias. Several high profile crimes in America have shaped our public policy. In the previous chapter on drugs, I discussed the country's knee jerk reaction to basketball star Len Bias' drug overdose. The same applies to our justice system. While it's been okay for African Americans to kill one another, it was the abduction and murder of White 12-year-old Polly Klaas in California that spurred America to get tough on crime. When there was a random shooting by an African American gunman on a Long Island commuter train, America again reacted and wanted to get tough on crime. The school shootings in Santee, Columbine, Colorado, Oregon, and Kentucky also triggered knee jerk criminal legislation.

No longer confined to the inner city, crime was officially part of the social landscape in affluent suburbs. Unfortunately, federal and state legislatures also succumbed to the hype. In 1994, in response to the death of Polly Klaas, California passed the infamous three strikes and you're out legislation. [70] Later, 36 additional states also passed similar three-strike legislation. Georgia and South Carolina have gone one step further and have created two strikes and you're out.

In this type of legislation, the third offense must be a felony in order to receive a life sentence. Nationwide, approximately 3,500 Americans have received life sentences for three-strike legislation. In California, 40,000 Americans, primarily Black and brown citizens, have been convicted. [71] In California, the third offense doesn't even have to be a felony. There have been numerous third strike minor offenses, such as stealing a slice of pizza, a roll of toilet tissue, or a bicycle. Numerous jurors in California have left the proceedings because, as they just told the judge, they could not send someone to jail for life for stealing a candy bar. There are horror stories nationwide in which two-time offenders had turned their lives around, committed a misdemeanor, and were sentenced for life.

This is the mean spirit that exists in America. In 1994, President Bill Clinton strengthened the existing Sentencing Reform Act of 1984 with the Federal Crime Bill. The purpose of these acts was to enforce America's desire to get tougher on crime. This legislation removed the option of parole for many offenders, and it forced the penal system to make offenders serve 85 percent of their time.

If an inmate has been sentenced to ten years in jail and a law requires that he endure 85 percent of that time, the system has literally negated any desire for the inmate to pursue rehabilitation and reduced time for good behavior. Most prisons don't provide rehabilitation for similar reasons. In 1995, the No-frills Act was passed. This bill took away most of the amenities that prisoners once possessed. This act denied inmates the opportunity to have a television in their cell. They could not have a computer in their cell and weight lifting equipment was removed. They could not make a telephone call without being monitored.

In 1996, the climate in prisons worsened with the passage of the Prison Litigation Reform Act. Prisons removed law libraries from most state and federal facilities. Prisoners were denied the right to file civil law suits. This meant that prisons could violate a prisoner's rights without the consequence of a civil suit. Prisoners could appeal to the local prison board, which is almost as ridiculous as having a police civilian review board monitor its own. The act also required a $120 filing fee, which, for most inmates, especially poor African American males, is a major hurdle. Inmates could only file a lawsuit three times. After that, the person was barred from further lawsuits and appeals.

In 1997, America again showed its true colors when it passed the Juvenile Crime Control Act. The government had already decided that 15 year-olds could be prosecuted as adults and placed in adult prisons. If that was not vicious enough, the new act allowed the justice department to try children as young as 13 years old as adults.

In the Dedication to this book, I mentioned Lionel Tate, the young African American teenager who, while imitating wrestling techniques on a six-year-old girl, killed her. Lionel, only 13 years old, was tried and convicted as an adult. Countries around the world do not view America as a first world country. How could a civilized society place a 13 year-old in jail with hardened criminals? African American youth have a six times greater chance of being prosecuted as an adult than White youth.

The Nathaniel Brazill case is another example of our misplaced values. I make no excuses for Nathaniel killing his teacher, but should a child be locked up with adults?

Have we dropped the word "rehabilitation" altogether? Which would cost the taxpayer less money: incarcerating someone for life or rehabilitating an inmate to help him become a law-abiding citizen who pays taxes?

BET Tonight reported on May 15, 2001, that the ratio of African American youth to White youth who are tried as adults is six to one. Ironically, when Nathaniel Abraham was being prosecuted as an adult, the son of a White police chief in a nearby Michigan town killed his sister. This White child was tried as a youth and the case received little media attention. The same holds true for White fifteen-year old Charles Williams, who killed two classmates and injured 13 others in a California school, yet he's being prosecuted as a youth.

You can tell a lot about a country by the way it treats its youth. In America, more than 100,000 youth of all races are in juvenile detention facilities. Almost 10,000 juveniles have been placed in adult facilities. Seventy-seven percent of juveniles placed in adult prisons are African American. [72] How do we reconcile the fact that African Americans are only 13 percent of the U.S. population, but constitute 77 percent of the youth placed in adult prisons? Can you imagine what it is like for a 13 year-old child who has to share a cell with a hardened criminal serving a life sentence without parole? These young people are like fresh meat to adults.

I do not defend Lionel Tate for killing a six year-old child. I do not defend the six year-old boy in Flint, Michigan, who killed a fellow six year-old classmate. I do not defend any youth who has killed or hurt people. However, I still must ask the question, what kind of people are we to place children in adult facilities? Why won't we rehabilitate them? What kind of outcome are we expecting when we place a 13-year-old in an adult facility for 25 years and they must serve 85 percent of their time? What kind of person will re-enter society?

There is legislation that says that if a juvenile is selling drugs a thousand feet from a school, he or she will be tried as an adult with the possibility of a life sentence without parole. In contrast, a juvenile selling near his or her home is treated as a juvenile. Consequently, a White youth selling drugs in his suburban neighborhood would be treated as a juvenile. An African American youth living in the inner city and within walking distance of his school, could be prosecuted as an adult and receive a life sentence if he was selling drugs.

When are we going to realize the error in of ways and properly match the punishment to the crime? One alternative to placing juveniles in adult facilities is boot camps. In the chapter on Solutions, I will discuss boot camps in more detail. While I have some concerns about boot camps, I do believe boot camps would be a far better solution than placing youth with hardened adult criminals.

In the previous chapter on drugs, we pointed out that in 1980, 581,000 people were arrested for drug possession. In 1990, the figure had doubled to more than a million. By the end of the 20th century, the figure had doubled again to close to two million arrests for drug possession. Is counting the number of arrests the best way to measure the war on drugs? As we pointed out in the last chapter, the war will not be won on the supply side, but on the side of demand. If America's goal is to incarcerate all people who are primarily Black, male, and poor and who are in possession of five grams of crack, this is going to be a very costly war, not only for the American tax payer but for African American males.

African American males are only six percent of the country's population, but for the first time in the history of the country are greater than 50 percent of the penal population. One in three African American males between the ages of 20 and 29 years of age are either in jail, on parole, or on probation. Sixty-one percent of all inmates are there because of drug-related crimes. In addition, drug-related crimes draw more jail time than more dangerous crimes. The following chart illustrates the concern.

Offense	Time Served
Drugs	78 Months
Fire Arms	69 Months
Sexual Abuse	68 Months
Assault	28 Months
Manslaughter	30 Months
Burglary	24 Months
Auto Theft	20 Months [73]

Do we really believe that Black, male, young, and poor Americans are incarcerated because they were in possession of five grams of crack cocaine? Is it fair to place a nonviolent inmate who was in possession of an illicit drug with murders, robbers, and sex offenders? Is it fair that the person who was in possession of five grams of crack cocaine should stay in jail longer than almost every other criminal except murderers? With three-strikes-you're-out sentencing, a person whose third crime was drug possession could actually stay in jail longer than murderers. This irrational behavior and inconsistency between punishment and crime contributes to this state of emergency.

The combination of the war on drugs and get tough on crime has had a more detrimental and deleterious effect on the African American community than slavery. I once thought that the Maafa, (the African Holocaust,) was the greatest tragedy on African people, but the war on drugs and get tough on crime have sunk our community into new depths of despair.

African Americans are also concerned about crime. We watch TV more than anyone else in America. People who know each other, look like each other, and live in the same neighborhood perpetrate most crime. This is often called Black-on-Black crime. The same holds true in any other community. African Americans have a first-hand view of the impact that crime has had on their community. Because drugs are illegal, therefore more costly, African Americans have had more cars, stereos, CD players, televisions and other forms of property stolen. Consequently, many African Americans also have a get tough on crime policy. By the year 2020, it is projected that two of every three African American males between the ages of 20 and 29 will be involved in the penal institution. We will have gone from one of ten, to two of three, in less than four decades.

We need leadership from the Black and White communities that will not be reactionary, self-centered, or short term. We need a long-term policy that will address the root causes of our incarceration problem. In the meantime, what has happened in America is an illusion of a war on drugs and the get tough on crime philosophy. White America is silent and Black America is overwhelmed.

Despite looming recessions, the prison industry continues to grow. From an investment perspective, there is no better place to invest than the prison industry. Just as slavery was good for America, prisons have been equally successful. Rural America and poor White Americans have become major beneficiaries. Prisons have become the great stimulator for a very depressed market in America.

In many rural towns throughout America, factories closed down and farms were foreclosed. How would the people survive? Years ago, rural towns began to compete for lucrative prison contracts.

Let me describe Crescent City, California, a town just like many rural communities whose better days had come and gone. Crescent City was fortunate enough to win the bid for the $277 million Pelican Bay State Prison. Crescent City went from being a ghost town to a boom town. The prison employs 1,500 people. The annual payroll is $50 million and the budget is $90 million. Indirectly, the prison has created work in everything from construction to pumping gas to domestic violence counseling. The contract for hauling prison garbage is worth $133,000 a year, big money in California's poorest county. Also cashing in on the action is a huge Ace Hardware, a private hospital, a 90,000 square feet K-Mart, which sells everything from toothpaste to Spice Girl paraphernalia. Across from K-Mart is an equally mammoth Safeway. Before the prison, the county collected $73 million in sales tax. Last year it collected

$142 million. In addition, the local government is saving money by using low security level one prisoners instead of public work crews. Pelican Bay inmates work almost 150,000 hours on everything from school grounds to public buildings. According to one report, the prison labor billed at a meager sum of $7.00 an hour, would have cost the county at least $766,000. [74]

Little towns and big prisons are a marriage made in heaven. The fodder comes from inner city Black communities and the beneficiaries are small White towns. Republicans represent 50 percent of the Senate, but Republican districts house 89 percent of America's prisons. When they say "lock em up," they mean in their district. The war on drugs and get tough on crime has become a boom for rural, low-income White America. Nationally, the tab for building penitentiaries has averaged about $7 billion annually over the last decade. Estimates for yearly expenses of incarceration run between $20 and $35 billion annually. One report found that 523,000 full-time employees work in American corrections facilities, more than any Fortune 500 company except General Motors. In the American countryside, punishment is such a big industry that according to the National Criminal Justice Commission, prisoners accounted for five percent of the growth and rural population between 1980 and 2000.

Today's prison industry has its own trade shows, mail order catalogues, newsletters, and conventions; literally thousands of corporations are dependent. At a typical trade show, 700 to 1,000 corporate vendors can be found standing amid a maze of neon signs, looking to get their piece of the pie. An army of corrections and law enforcement officials are awarded, wined and dined by lobbyists.

The Penal System

Since 1990, the United States has been constructing enough prison facilities to hold an average of 92,640 new beds per year and these beds are not cheap. As of 1998, the cost for creating a new maximum-security bed was $70,909, for medium security it was $49,853 per bed, and for minimum security the price was $29,311 for each bed added. This incredible amount of money being poured in the prisons has lured some of the biggest construction firms in the world into the business; among them are Turner Construction, Brown & Root, and CRSS. Underwriting prison construction by selling tax-exempt bonds is now estimated to be a $3 billion annual industry. [75]

Another piece of the prison industrial complex is the exploitation of prison labor by private and state-owned companies. Convict labor is seen as efficient and economical. Senator Phil Graham said, "I want to turn every federal prison in this country into a mini industrial park." Already American convicts toil for private firms making copper faucets, blue jeans, circuit boards for nuclear power plants, and stretch limousines. In San Diego, prisoners working for CMT Blues tear Made in Honduras labels off T-shirts and replace them with labels reading made in the USA. Other convicts take reservations for TWA, work at telemarketing and data entry, and slaughter ostriches for export to Europe. Prison labor is used to package everything from Microsoft Windows 95 and 98 to Starbucks coffee products to Jans Sport Gear. Subcontractors for Eddie Bauer and Victoria's Secret have also used inmate workers. Meanwhile in Louisiana, CCA has teamed up with a world clothes manufacturer company.[76] This makes for strange bed partners.

The largest single employer of prison labor with 18,000 making 150 different products is Federal Prison Industries, also known as Unicor. The company is state-owned and can sell only to other federal agencies, but those markets are guaranteed carved out for Unicor by law. Currently Unicor makes everything from safety goggles and wiring for air force fighter jets to body armor for the border patrol and road signs for the park service. In 1998, the firm produced $512 million in goods and services. [77] Given all this hard work going on in the big house it would appear that America's two million prisoners are becoming a third world within; a cheap and bountiful labor reservoir already being tapped by big business and Uncle Sam alike.

Frederick Douglass taught us years ago that power concedes nothing without a struggle. This prison industry has now become big business. The war on drugs and get tough on crime not only is a misguided, incorrect policy, but it has also created two lucrative industries: the DEA and the penal industry. The beneficiaries (and they are numerous) need Black inmates in order to keep the industry thriving.

In my closing chapter, we will look at what it will take to dismantle this industry. Too many White families in rural American communities are benefiting from Black male prisoners for them to have compassion. Too many businesses and municipalities are benefiting to show compassion. The Fortune 500 corporations and large construction companies have too much at stake financially for them to consider a more compassionate approach. Not only has the private sector become more involved in the penal industry, but also private corporations have now positioned themselves with the government to actually house prisoners.

The two largest are Correction Corporations of America and Wackenhut. Were these companies hired because they could save the government money? Were they hired to reduce the recidivism rate? Did they have a better rehabilitation program? Were the facilities better? Was the staff better trained? The answer to all of these questions is no. The General Accounting Office found that public and private prisons cost taxpayers roughly the same. For example, a Louisiana study found that the average inmate cost per day for the two private facilities studied were $23.75 and a comparable daily operational cost for the public facility study was $23.55 per inmate. [78]

Private prisons make money by cutting corners by means of skimping on food, staffing, medicine, education, and other services for convicts. It also means fielding poorly trained, ill equipped, non-unionized, and often brutal guards. Exploitation of staff leads to high turnover rate, while the drive to keep overhead low means that many open positions remain vacant for months. One private prison in Florida, according to state audits, had an annual staff turnover rate of 200 percent. [79] Private prisons also achieve economies of scale by eliminating labor through specially designed, automated, hands-off prisons. The design of the control room will enable a guard to simultaneously watch three pods of 250 prisoners each. Windows in an elevated room form an unobstructive view of each cell block below and vision blocks in the floor are positioned over each entranceway so guards can visually identify anyone being admitted. The high tech panel at the center of the room can open any door at the flick of a switch. Such futuristic profit pins are built to function with no more than five guards controlling 750 inmates, or at least that seems to be the plan.

The first political rumbling from within the bowels of the CCA empire came on clouds of pepper spray and smoke in the summer of 1995. Prisoners from North Carolina, homesick, ill treated, and packed into a house of corrections, trashed and burned two of their dorms. The riot lasted several hours and was only put down when CCA's overwhelmed guards finally handed over operations to local swat commandos. The facility in question was actually nothing more than a Motel 6 retrofitted with bars, bunks, and fences. Packed into tiny rooms with no access to exercise or other activities, the detainees endured months on end of stultifying boredom, bad food, smelly toilets, and humiliation at the hands of CCA staff.

On June 18, 1995, desperation peaked; the 300 detainees finally exploded, trashing their rooms, smashing toilets, and burning mattresses. The next month brought a cascade of revelations and inquiries. It seemed CCA's rent-a-cop security force was not only ill equipped and poorly trained, but battered by employee racism and reckless penny pinching. The new prison was so unsafe, the staff was soon deserting in droves. CCA had deliberately passed on firearms training because state certification cost up to $3,000 per person. A later report by the GOA found, among other things, that 80 percent of the CCA guards had no correction experience. Many of the guards were only 18 or 19 years old. Prison medical records were unaccounted for, and more than 200 chronically ill inmates were left untreated in the general population, and almost no effort was made to separate violent psychos from peaceful convicts. [80]

Later, inmate civil rights suits alleged that the guards violated regulations by using tear gas inside. The prison tactical teams dragged inmates naked and shackled across floors. During cell searches convicts were forced to strip, and were shot with stun guns if they moved. One female clerical worker told her roommate, "The guards here are like people who got beat up in high school and this was their way of getting back at the world."

The No Frills Act of 1995, reinforced what the public and private sectors were doing in the prison industry. The result is more than 300,000 inmates annually are raped and many are raped daily. [81] Robert Duman, a mental health clinician with the Massachusetts Department of Corrections, sighted that young prisoners' chances of avoiding rape in an adult facility are almost zero. "He'll get raped within the first 24 or 48 hours; that's almost standard." Prisons are commonly referred to as punk factories, and many prison guards use male rapists to do their dirty work.

In the age of AIDS, prison rape is like Russian roulette, which makes it a terrifying weapon. As one HIV positive prison rape survivor put it, "No where in the book of rules was it written that I had to get raped, destroy my mind, and get AIDS." While AIDS has been declining in the White gay community, it has been increasing in the African American community, outstripping homicide, and has become the number one killer among African American males. [82] Because of the AIDS epidemic, Surgeon General David Satcher recommends condom distribution to inmates while incarcerated and upon their release. Forty-seven percent of new male HIV cases are African Americans.

AIDS is now the number two killer among African American women after heart disease. Sixty-three percent of HIV women are African American. The increasing number of African American males incarcerated in "punk factories," being violated by male rapists, engaging in conjugal visits, and having sex when released has contributed to the AIDS epidemic in the African American community.

Various reports estimate that between 20 and 30 percent of inmates will be raped while incarcerated. If there are approximately 1.5 million African American males incarcerated and 30 percent of them are raped, we are looking at a figure of 450,000 African American males. HIV prevalence among prisons has exploded in recent years with the rate of infection nearly 13 times that of the non-prison population. [83] This is a state of emergency.

In addition, some estimate that 15 percent of all inmates are suffering from mental illness. To house nonviolent offenders, drug users, and juveniles with inmates who are mentally ill is barbaric and absurd. You would not expect this from a first world country. In New York State, there have been incidents of tuberculosis, which has spread throughout the inmate population, and this is not an anomaly. As the prison population ages (thanks to previously sighted legislation), more inmates will require medical assistance. This was a problem in public prisons; you can imagine what they will receive in private prisons.

The mean spirit has showed its ugly head in another form with the reinstitution of chain gangs. They were used during slavery and reconstruction, but were abolished in the 1960s. Twenty thousand members of the American Correctional Association, comprised primarily of wardens, oppose chain gangs. The ACLU also opposes chain gangs and says it violates the 13th Amendment. Many states have considered implementing chain gangs. Five states have actually implemented them. The first in 1995 was Alabama followed by Florida, Arizona, Wisconsin, and Iowa.

Prisoners are either shackled together or chains are placed around both of their legs and they primarily work in very visible public arenas, i.e. the town square. And, if prisoners do not agree to work on the chain gang, they are forced to fulfill 100 percent of their sentence versus 85 percent. This in reality becomes no choice at all. Guards are instructed to shoot to kill. Many guards have viewed this as an opportunity for shooting practice. Amnesty International, which also disapproves of the United States role in chain gangs, says the practice violates the international law that the United States ratified in 1992. A year after chain gangs were implemented in 1995, Alabama decided it was not the best way to treat criminals.

Maryland decided that rather than using chain gangs, they would use a stun belt and empower the inmate with a 50,000-volt surge if there were any violations.[84] This is not a pretty picture for America, but with get tough on crime and television murder news, the environment is ripe to pass inhumane legislation.

In my opinion, the most barbaric act is the death penalty. America is a very interesting company; Iran, Pakistan, Saudi Arabia, and Yemen are just some of the few remaining countries that believe in the death penalty. One hundred and six countries, including almost all of Europe and even South Africa, have abolished the death penalty. Since 1979, 697 Americans have been executed. America is one of the few countries that execute children. One hundred and sixty children have been executed in America. The youngest was 14-year-old George Stinney in the state of South Carolina.[85] As of January 1, 2001, 3,726 Americans were waiting on death row. Forty-three percent were African Americans.

Isn't it ironic that politicians run their campaign promoting Christianity and pro life, yet those same politicians are in full support of the death penalty? Politicians read polls and are very much aware that a Harris Poll (July 13, 2000) found that 64 percent of Americans were in favor of the death penalty. A Gallup Poll (August 29, 2000) found that 67 percent of Americans were in favor of the death penalty. [86] Unfortunately, the policy on the death penalty is not well thought out and is being driven by the media.

Ironically, while the American public is in favor of the death penalty, 82 percent of law officials do not believe it is an effective deterrent to crime. [87] Dane Archer and Rosemary Gartner studied 110 nations from 1900–1970 and found the death penalty had no deterrence to the homicide rate. An Ohio study determined the greater the punishment the shorter the time before the person was rearrested.

The five countries with the highest homicide rate and no death penalty averaged 21 homicides per 100,000. The five countries with the highest homicide rates but have the death penalty, which includes the United States, have a median number of 42 homicides per 100,000. [88] In addition, a death penalty case will cost the American taxpayer up to $3 million in litigation. Even a life sentence would only cost $500,000. The death penalty is not a deterrent to crime, is not supported by law enforcement, and is not cost effective.

The Columbia School of Law reviewed cases between 1973 and 1995 and found that 66 percent of the verdicts were flawed and the two primary reasons were incompetent lawyers and law enforcement officials suppressing evidence. [89] Less than eight percent of all lawyers are involved with criminal law. Moreover, of the 800,000 United States lawyers, less than one percent represents the indigent accused. In the African American community, the death penalty is even more significant because 43 percent of the death row inmates are African American. Professors David Baldus, George Woodworth, and Charles Paulaski conducted the most exhaustive study of the racial breakdown of the death penalty. They studied more than 2,000 murder cases in Georgia in the 1970s. Baldus and his colleagues found that defendants charged with killing White victims received the death penalty 11 times more often than defendants charged with killing Black victims. Black defendants charged with killing White victims received a death sentence 22 percent of the time while White defendants charged with killing Black victims received the death penalty in only three percent of the cases. [90]

In Illinois, Governor George Ryan, after reviewing his own state's death penalty accuracy of only 50 percent, decided that until he was absolutely sure that the state could guarantee 100 percent, placed a moratorium on executions in the state of Illinois. President Bush said that while governor of Texas, he was confident that he and the state had never made a mistake! The problem for the remaining part of the country is that Bill Clinton signed a Death Penalty Act, which practically eliminates the right of habeas corpus by shortening the process of one year. The average length of time needed for a person to be proven innocent on death row is between six and ten years, but many cases take considerably longer.

It suffices to say that if the death penalty cannot be dispensed with equity and absolute certainty of guilt, it should not be dispensed at all. I believe most Americans would agree with this principal, but polls continue to show public support of the death penalty. Americans only hear one side of the story.

The media and our elected officials rarely discuss inequalities in our justice system. In fact, less than three percent of all crime coverage ever examines the court proceedings. Instead, the media chooses to focus almost entirely on the sensational aspect of a murder to generate profits. Obviously after being bombarded with one emotional bloody image after another, coupled with heart wrenching testimonies by a victim's loved one, it is nearly impossible for the public to be concerned about the accused of such heinous crimes.

Throughout this chapter, I have mentioned many legislative acts that have had a tremendous affect on our penal system and specifically African American males. There is one piece of legislation that is still being considered in the Congress and I would encourage all of you to contact your local Representative to pass the Innocence Protection Act. The objective is to reduce the number of innocent persons that are put to death. The bill will ensure that convicted offenders are afforded an opportunity to prove their innocence through DNA testing, to help states provide competent legal services, and to inform jurors about sentencing options. Several states have passed or are considering legislation while they wait for federal support. The term "capital punishment" means just that in America; if you have capital, you have a much greater chance of not receiving punishment. If O.J. Simpson had not received "dream team" legal representation, his verdict probably would have been different.

Throughout this book, we have talked about the significance of race and age, but now I want to enter the variable of class. In America, one-third of the African American population lives below the poverty line while only one-tenth of the White community lives in poverty. While on the aggregate there are more Whites living below the poverty line (24 million), on a percentage basis it's not close. Eighty percent of defendants charged with felonies in the country's 75 largest counties were indigent. Approximately three-quarters of all inmates in state prisons were represented by public defenders or some other publicly provided attorney. [91]

Without such assistance most criminal defendants would go unrepresented. The significance of the Innocence Protection Act is that the quality of defense that is given to low-income people, primarily people of color and specifically African American males, is a pale comparison to the quality of the prosecution. As long as the state provides a warm body with a law degree and bar admission, little else matters. Indigent defense council are generally underpaid, overworked, and given insufficient resources to conduct an adequate investigation and defense.

Although the Supreme Court formerly requires that the defense council provide effective assistance, it has set the standard for effectiveness so low that even lawyers who are drunk, asleep, or have been disbarred have been deemed effective. The average number of hours to try a criminal case ranges between 300 and 600 hours. If the state only allocates $1,000 for defense representation, and we divide $1,000 by 500 hours, we're talking about a lawyer being paid $2 per hour. I think O.J.'s dream team was paid a little more than $2 per hour. A national law journal study of 20 randomly chosen Alabama death penalty trials found the average length of trial to be 4.2 days, with the penalty phase lasting an average of only 3.6 hours. Compare that to how the dream team stretched the trial for O.J., you gain a greater perspective for the performance of a good legal defense. By contrast, when a defense attorney demonstrates competence and dedication, he can find it difficult to get appointed for precisely that reason. Trial courts consistently refuse to appoint competent defense attorneys.

DNA testing was a tremendous factor for O.J. Simpson, along with many of the victims that were on death row erroneously. Historically, the cost of DNA testing has ranged between $5,000 and $10,000. Technological advances have reduced the cost to $100. New York and Illinois have a ten-month backlog of DNA cases while victims wait for the test. In California there are 115,000 inmates who cannot post bail while they are waiting for DNA testing.

Presently, jury discrimination is rampant. African American jurors are removed five times more than Whites. We will never know, but it appears O.J. Simpson benefited from the racial make-up of the jury in Los Angeles and his lawyers were quick to make sure there was a racial balance in that jury. African Americans need to appreciate jury selection. In Chicago, 60 percent of African Americans don't respond to jury duty while only eight percent of White Americans are negligent.

Before I provide some solutions to the penal system in this chapter and more in the Solutions chapter, I wanted to look at some geographical differences in America. While all 50 states and the District of Columbia have failed African Americans, some states are far worse than others. Texas has to be considered one of the worse states for African Americans. One of every 25 African Americans is an inmate. More Americans are executed there than in any other state. Texas is one of 14 states that either permanently or delays African Americans the right to vote.

California is a very close second. California has the most stringent interpretation of three strikes legislation and is the worst offender. It's also one of the 36 states that still believes in the death penalty, and is one of the 46 states that deny African Americans the right to vote.

Florida still believes in chain gangs. Thirty-one percent of African American males in the state (200,000) are denied the opportunity to vote. They easily could have helped Gore win the election. They are one of five states that constitute 42 percent of all death penalty executions along with Texas, Virginia, Missouri, and Oklahoma. Georgia believes in two strikes and you're out. South Carolina, who also believes in two strikes, executed the youngest person in the history of the country, a 14 year-old boy.

Kentucky allocates only $162 for an indigent defender. That came to $11 million, which was $4 million less than the University of Kentucky allocated for their athletic budget in the year 2000. Kentucky also believes in the death penalty and denies inmates the right to vote. While Minnesota has a very small percentage of African Americans, no state has a greater ratio of Black to White being incarcerated. The ratio in Minnesota is 23 to one.

While no states, in my opinion, receive an A, I do want to acknowledge Indiana, which is one of the few states to adopt rigorous standards for appointment of defense council in death penalty cases. Beginning in 1991, Indiana required appointment of two experienced attorneys in every capital case. The lead council must have at least five years of criminal trial experience, and must have been lead or co-council on five completed felony jury trials and one death penalty case. The other lawyer must have three years of trial experience and was lead or co-council on at least three complete felony trials. To be eligible for such appointment, lawyers must complete 12 hours of capital litigation training every other year. Lawyers are paid at least $70 per hour. Judges must ensure they are not overloaded with other cases, and public defenders may not be assigned any additional cases in the months preceding a capital trial. The Illinois Supreme Court has just required similar standards.

I pray that other states consider implementing these kinds of standards. I also want to commend Alaska, Hawaii, Iowa, Maine, Massachusetts, Michigan, Minnesota, North Dakota, Rhode Island, Vermont, West Virginia, Wisconsin, and the District of Columbia in not implementing the death penalty. In addition, I want to commend four states that do not take away inmates' right to vote (even though three of the states have very few African American males and the last has just a small percentage). Those states include Maine, Vermont, Utah, and Massachusetts. There are 46 states that deny four million inmates the right to vote of which 1.4 million are African American. Thirteen percent of African American males are disenfranchised. Ten states permanently bar inmates from voting, and that illustrious list includes Alabama, Florida, Iowa, Mississippi, New Mexico, Virginia, Wyoming, Delaware, Nevada, and Pennsylvania.

I am very much aware that the major hindrance to solving these problems is not sociological. It has nothing to do with our understanding of crime reduction, but the fact that crime does pay and pays very well. So at the very outset, we have diabolical interests. There are people in this country that have a vested interest in the maintenance of the status quo, which is to increase the penal population. On the other hand, I am very much committed to the reduction in the number of inmates and specifically African American males.

Within that context, my solutions are presented in the order that is more palatable for the ruling class of this country. The first would be eradication of the death penalty. This should be a little easier to sell because, if for no other reason, life imprisonment equates to $500,000. I mentioned earlier that it costs $3 million in litigation. The major obstacle on the eradication of the death penalty is changing public opinion that hovers near 65 percent. We need the media to show it is not cost-effective or a deterrent, and it makes us look very bad to the United Nations.

Second, we must separate the 10,000 juveniles who are currently placed in adult facilities. This requires no money. We're not talking about reducing the number of inmates; we're simply separating youth from adults. Earlier, we stated that the number of rapes and AIDS epidemic could be greatly reduced if we separated youth from adults. It's the humane thing to do and we would gain respect from the United Nations and alleviate further damage to our youth.

Third, we need to separate nonviolent offenders from violent offenders. Again, this does not require any additional money. The same number of inmates would be incarcerated; they'd just be placed in different facilities. Seven percent of the inmates commit 70 percent of the crimes. Why should a person who was simply guilty of being in possession of five grams of crack cocaine be incarcerated with a murderer? What is happening in many of our facilities is that inmates are going to crime school. They are learning tricks of the trade from murderers, burglars, and sexual offenders and when released, we become their new victim.

Fourth, we should increase the amount an inmate is given upon his or her release into society. Presently inmates receive a whopping grand total of $250. That would not provide one night's lodging at most New York hotels. Nor would it not provide one month's rent, much less food and other expenditures. Earlier in this chapter, we mentioned Unicorp and other private corporations that are using penal labor to provide a host of products and services. The least we could do is pay the inmate $10 for each day of his or her stay in prison. For example, $10 times 3,650 days (10 years) would be $35,500. This would be placed in his account and upon release would be provided. I would also suggest that the inmate not receive the money in cash, but certificates payable toward college tuition, rent, transportation, and entrepreneurship.

Another solution is geared primarily toward California. Forty thousand inmates in California are victims of three strikes legislation. California is the only state where a simple misdemeanor committed as a third offense can create a lifetime sentence. If California wants to remain one of the leading states in America, they must rescind this draconian law. Many of the men who are now in jail for life because they stole pizza were once taxpayers and caring fathers. California is losing more and more money with them being incarcerated.

Every state needs to emulate Indiana in death penalty representation. Every defendant needs proper representation. We are the laughing stock of the world, first because we still have the death penalty, but second because defendants (e.g., Kentucky) only receive $142 to defend themselves. We could also reduce the $3 million spent by the prosecution with competent, well-paid defense lawyers who could show their clients' innocence much earlier in the litigation process.

Inmates should also be enfranchised. This requires no money. In the last election between Bush and Gore, the world saw that America makes a mockery of the word democracy. Former President Jimmy Carter said that to ensure fair elections, irregularities should not exceed two percent. In America the figure was three percent. Not only is that a disparaging commentary on our democracy, but also to have four million Americans denied the opportunity to vote because they committed a crime is unacceptable. Thirteen percent of African American males are disfranchised, and this borders on barbarism. [92] If America is going to be the world leader it must model democracy. Those 46 states that deny inmates the opportunity to vote need to pass enfranchisement legislation. Those 14 states that continue to deny inmates who have served their time illustrate the mean spirit in America.

We need a more responsible and diversified media. Nine corporations in America literally control 90 percent of the flow of news in this country and much of the world. While we understand that budgets have been cut and the reporters are few, one station could exclusively focus on positive news, or feature more positive news and curtail the reporting of murders. In addition, news departments should allow regular features by institutions like the Rand Corporation. One 1997 Rand study documents that drug treatment was 15 times more successful at reducing crime than incarceration. [93] Another Rand study found that every dollar invested in substance abuse treatment generated $7 in savings, primarily through reductions in crime and reduced hospitalizations. Research also shows that we are spending $25,000 to incarcerate an inmate with a recidivism rate as high as 85 percent in the African American community. Yet it only costs $3,500 for drug treatment and $6,500 for intense probation. [94] The media needs to promote these studies.

Unfortunately, many prisons have dropped the word rehabilitation. Much of our current crime legislation does not encourage the prison or the inmate toward rehabilitation. In addition, the private sector, which is running more and more prisons, has no financial incentive for rehabilitation. The American public needs to understand they are not getting the most for their dollar. They are spending between $18,000 and $38,000 per inmate, with a recidivism rate that fluctuates between 40 percent and 85 percent, depending upon the state and the ethnicity of the inmate.

Releasing an illiterate inmate into society with all of $250, who has not learned any skills other than more crime strategies, is totally insane. Financial incentives rewarding reduced recidivism rates should be extended to private prisons. Prisons that improve literacy should be paid accordingly. More money should be allocated to employment training. Every inmate needs to learn how to read, type, master algebra, become computer literate, and improve communication and critical thinking skills. Head Start, Chapter I, and Pell Grants remain more cost effective than prisons.

Jerome Miller in the excellent book, *Search and Destroy* recommends that we prevent prosecutors from using their convictions to propel their political careers. Prosecutors should be appointed and prevented from running for any other political office. In addition, Miller suggests that paying informers $1 billion over the past 15 years has been a detriment to the criminal justice system. We have too many innocent victims in jail because the justice system used these unreliable, biased sources to incriminate innocent victims. The level of unity in the Black community already had a lot to be desired without planting these seeds of mistrust.

Once again, legislation is being considered to use the death penalty. This time it would be used for any gang member who killed witnesses. Besides the fact that the word gang can be subjective, some people believe if two or three African American males are standing on a corner, that act, in and of itself would constitutes a gang. Would this exempt the mafia? What is the difference between the mafia, the KKK, racial hate crime organizations, and gangs?

The above does not negate my concern for the protection of witnesses. Presently, society seems to be expecting witnesses to become martyrs. Oftentimes, witnesses do not come forth because they have first hand experience of observing witnesses and their families threatened, injured, killed, and their property destroyed. Law enforcement officials must do better. They must protect witnesses the way they would protect their own relatives. But more importantly, America is willing to consider the death penalty, which is extremely costly in litigation rather than provide better protection, relocation, housing, and employment.

Why would anyone risk their life, be relocated from family and friends, lose their home and job, and have their children transferred from their schools? America is willing to spend thousands of dollars on death penalty litigation, but will not offer witnesses financial incentives to testify. I recommend that $100,000 is provided for corroborated testimony incentives. I also recommend that gang members, mafia organizations, the KKK and other groups who attempt to intimidate witnesses (much less kill them) will receive life imprisonment, without any chance of parole.

My last solution will be more difficult to sell. We need to abolish private prisons. The cost per day in a private prison is no cheaper than in a public prison. Private prisons provide inadequate services and everyone is at risk. Private prisons create an atmosphere designed for animals, not humans. When you bring the profit motive into the penal industry you are asking for cannibalistic behavior. Of course, I am very much aware that this solution goes against the financial interest of the CCA, Wackenhut, Unicorp, and numerous other private companies that have benefited off the backs of inmates. But taxpayers need to realize that they cannot continue to pay $18,000 to 32,000 to private corporations and not receive a return on their money.

As a result of the prison state in America, we will look in the next chapter on its impact to fathers.

**TATE**

OF

**MERGENCY**

FATHERLESSNESS

Men often ask me if I have any good news to tell. When I preach a men's day sermon, brothers welcome the fact that I accentuate the positive. There's nothing worse than for good Black men who are trying to do the right thing for their families, to listen to a preacher talk about how bad Black men are.

In my book *Good Brothers Looking for Good Sisters,* I describe six positive brothers, one of whom is a single parent. Raymond's wife died in labor and he has chosen not to remarry. Diane is now six years old, and she is the apple of her father's eye. Raymond would do anything for Diane, and the bond between Raymond and Diane is newsworthy. You can look into his eyes and see unconditional love for his child. You can look into Diane's eyes and you can see total trust and admiration for her daddy.

Raymond represents more than 400,000 African American males who quietly raise their sons and daughters by themselves. [95] In the previous chapter, we showed how the media distorts news, and 43 percent of local news covers violence. Wouldn't it be nice if the opening news story would cover one of these 400,000 African American males who starts the day by waking his children, braiding his daughter's hair, preparing his children's breakfast, walking or driving his children to school, going on to work, making provisions for after school care, picking them up, returning home to make dinner, checking homework, playing a board game and sharing a Bible story before going to sleep. Raymond is that kind of parent.

A friend of mine named Roscoe told me that as he, his wife, and two children were touring the Museum of Science and Industry in Chicago, he noticed that people kept looking at him strangely. He looked at his children to see if there was something wrong with them—maybe their shoestrings were untied or there was something wrong with their clothing—everything seemed fine. He then looked at his wife to see if she had spilled pop or something, but she seemed okay. Then he looked at himself and thought maybe when he was eating he had spilled catsup on his shirt, but that was not the problem. It continued to puzzle him for the next hour as they continued to enjoy the museum. He asked his wife, "Have you noticed people are looking at us?" His wife quickly commented, "You didn't know? You are the only African American male in the museum!" There were only four other African American families in the museum, all without a father. This puzzled Roscoe because with more than 4,000 visitors in the museum, it hadn't dawned on him that he was the only African American male.

Wherever Roscoe and his family went—the zoo, aquarium, planetarium, or library—he noticed the same thing. This has become a state of emergency.

We need fathers who will stay with their children. What do Tiger Woods, Shaq, Michael Jordan, and Venus and Serena Williams have in common? Beyond their talents and supportive mothers, they all had fathers who were driving forces in their lives. I challenge all fathers to learn from these great men. We need fathers who will take their children places. There are fathers who have stayed with their wives and children, but for some reason, don't feel it's in their job description to take trips. When sons are raised in households where fathers are non-participants, they're learning from example about the diminished role African American men play in families.

I am often asked what I feel is the greatest problem facing Black America. Many believe the greatest problem is racism. They document that we were forced to come to America, separated from our family, made to work free of charge from 1619 to 1865, and never given reparations. We were told that we were free, but free to do what? Free to go where?

Some feel the greatest problem facing African American people is monopoly capitalism, which creates poverty. Some feel the greatest problem facing Black America is spirituality, the lack of morality in the African American community. My wife believes the greatest problem is that many of our people are not saved. They have not allowed the Lord Jesus to order their steps. Others feel the greatest problem facing the Black family is fatherlessness. The lack of men in the home has reached epidemic proportions. It has become a state of emergency.

In 1920, 90 percent of our youth had fathers at home. In 1960, 80 percent of our youth had their fathers at home, but in 2001, only 30 percent of our youth have their fathers at home. [96] If we understand the history of this country and racism, how do we reconcile that 301 (1619–1920) years after slavery, reconstruction, and Jim Crow, 90 percent of African American children still had their fathers in the home? As significant as racism is on the African American community, slavery and racism did not separate African American men from their children as late as 1920. Even as late as 1960 with monopoly capitalism and poverty, 80 percent of African American fathers remained at home with their children. Something happened in Black America between 1960 and the new millennium and it has had a deleterious effect on the African American family.

We will have to critically look at the disease of fatherlessness if we are going to save the Black family. I am not trying to minimize racism or poverty, but I am concerned that we spend a lot more time pointing the finger at our oppressor and very little time looking at what we as men can do to stay at home with our children. I would also like to see just as much attention given to Black-on-Black male violence and murder as racial hate crimes. Last year, Black-on-Black male violence occurred more than 6,000 times; racial hate crimes occurred less than 20 times. We can start with the rash of murders in Cincinnati. Racism may be the problem, but we will be the solution.

We have lived in America for almost 400 years. Historian Ivan Van Sertima documents in *They Came Before Columbus* that we had traveled here as early as 800 B.C., well before Columbus got lost and invaded the Native Americans.

What happened between 1960 and 2000, a brief 40 years that could have had such a detrimental effect on the African American family? Did racism become greater, more overt? Did Black men attend church less between 1960 and 2000? Was there less Bible study in these last four decades? In my book *Adam, Where Are You?* I discussed the fact that unfortunately, most churches have many more females than males in their congregations. Did more African American males attend church in the years before 1960?

Fatherlessness

We live in a country that is capitalistic and patriarchal. It is very difficult for a man to be a man in America without income. A people without a future are dangerous. Humans lacking goals, who have nothing to lose, make foolish mistakes. Male readers, ask yourself, if you lost your job, how long would you be able to maintain your present level of self-esteem? I've been told between three and 12 months. Too often, successful African American males cannot comprehend the effect of being unemployed, underemployed, and illiterate in the richest country in the world. I also asked women how long would they stay with their husbands if they were unemployed. Many women said they wouldn't stay too long.

In a capitalistic country, if you lack capital you are considered worthless. It has also been said that a man is evaluated on his level of productivity. In Black America many of our men are not productive. Drive through any inner city community and you will see young, able bodied, intelligent African American males hanging idly on street corners. This was not the case in 1619, 1700, 1865, 1920, or 1954. African people were brought to this country to work. Does that reason exist today? Well, let's look at the facts.

In the 1990s when America had great economic growth, Black male unemployment did not drop below ten percent. While the economy was soaring, America was also placing a record number of African American males in jail. From a cynical perspective I could say, that may be why White America needs Black males to continue the fastest growth industry—prisons.

America has gone through three distinct economic periods. The first was agriculture. That was the major reason why African people were brought to this country, to work farms. Ironically, Africans were accused of being lazy. If we were lazy then why did White Americans travel three months on a slave ship named Jesus and three months to return us to America if we were lazy? If White Americans had such a great work ethic they should have worked America.

From 1619 to 1900, America's economy was driven by agriculture. Black men were needed and productive, therefore Black men stayed with their families. From 1900 to 1960, America moved into manufacturing. Black men were needed to work in factories. Black men were productive and stayed with their families. From 1960 to the present, America has moved from manufacturing to the information age. The U.S. has moved from the farm to the factory to the computer. There is now less need for African Americans, specifically African American males.

It has been said that racism is irrational. It appears that America does not need Black labor, yet there is a shortage of 350,000 computer programmers. America is willing to import foreigners to fill these positions rather than educate African American males.

In a country that is capitalistic and patriarchal, it is very difficult to propose marriage to someone when you're unemployed. If you don't believe that, become unemployed and propose to your special someone and see what kind of response you'll receive. It is very difficult to propose to someone while incarcerated. It is very difficult to propose to someone when you're illiterate. It is very difficult to propose to someone when your first lover is crack cocaine. It is very frustrating proposing and staying married to someone when you are denied equal access to housing, earn less, and pay more. It is very difficult to propose and stay married to someone when you're constantly having to train inexperienced, less qualified Whites to be your supervisor.

Fatherlessness

These are some factors that contribute to the high rate of fatherlessness in African American families. Only 30 percent of African American children have their fathers at home. If racism ended tomorrow, would the percentage of African American men staying with their children increase? If we receive reparations next week, would the percentage of at-home African American fathers return to the 90 percent figure we had in 1920?

What separates a man from his wife? What separates a man from his children? In White America the divorce rate is 50 percent. In White America, between one-third and one-half of White children also live in homes where the father is absent. Do White fathers leave because of racism? Would reparations bring them back? The issue is deeper than racism and economics. Why do so many fathers abandon their children when they divorce the wife? Seldom do you see a wife divorce her husband and simultaneously divorce herself from her children. Some would say the reason why the bond is greater between mother and child is because the mother carried the child for nine months. If the mother breastfed her babies, the bond is even greater. How can a man divorce his wife and children, shack with another woman, and spend more time and money with her child than his own? Why don't women encourage men to take a more active role in the growth and development of their biological children? That is the demon of selfishness and self-centeredness. God will not be mocked. You will reap whatever you sow. Shacking females will eventually see him turn against her.

If racism ended tomorrow and we received reparations shortly thereafter, if Black men became literate and computer savvy, if they were no longer incarcerated, if they earned what White men earn, would that eliminate fatherlessness? Are all unemployed, underemployed, illiterate, drug addicted, and incarcerated fathers abandoning their children? Are all educated, employed African American men staying at home with their children? I don't think so. Racism and economics cannot explain fully this disease of fatherlessness.

I believe the greatest problem facing Black America is not racism, economics, or fatherlessness, but the lack of a personal relationship with Jesus Christ. Notice I did not say the greatest problem is that men do not go to church. What I am saying is that the greatest problem facing Black men is that they do not have a personal relationship with and are not in constant fellowship with the Lord Jesus Christ. A man who makes Jesus Christ his example is a man who will be incapable of ever abandoning his children.

There is a tremendous difference between salvation and fellowship. Once a decision for Christ is made, salvation is instant. Fellowship is an on-going process that lasts forever. I have truly upped the anti on this issue because in Black America we have a problem with the number and percentage of men in church, much less a percentage of men who are saved, and even less a percentage of men in regular fellowship with Jesus Christ.

In my best seller *Adam, Where Are You?* I listed 21 reasons why Black men do not go to church. Satan knows the most effective way to destroy the family, Black or White, is to separate the man from God. A man separated from God is a man with no power. A man separated from God is a dangerous man. He lives to satisfy the flesh and not the spirit. A man separated from God is a man who would leave his children. The demon that is driving fatherlessness is not racism; just ask White men. The demon driving fatherlessness is not a change in economy; just ask all the gainfully employed men who are not taking care of their children.

The demon driving fatherlessness is a separation between God and man. Satan knows that when you save a man you save a family. Satan knows that some women will compromise and marry a man who has not committed his life to the Lord Jesus. She makes the daughter go to church but not the son. In my book, "Countering the Conspiracy to Destroy Black Boys", I mention that some mothers raise their daughters and love their sons. Are some boys learning to be pimps from their mothers? Do boys shack and men marry? Some women compromise, but Satan knows that men do not compromise. Satan knows that men who are sold out to Jesus are not as prone to compromise. They will almost always marry saved women who too are committed to the Savior. If the man is in relationship everyone is going to church, the wife, the daughter, the son, the dog, the cat, the roaches, everyone goes when the man is in relationship. A man in regular fellowship with God does not abandon his children. In the future, God willing, I plan to write *What Happens When A Man Meets Jesus*. In this book I will look at what happens to a man whose mind has been renewed to conform with God's word.

David Blankenhorn's book, *Fatherless in America*, takes an excellent look at fatherlessness from a secular perspective. He says,

> "In a larger sense the fatherhood story is the irreplaceable basis of culture's most urgent imperative: the socialization of males. More than other culture interventions, fatherhood guides men away from violence by fashioning their behavior to a fundamental

social purpose. By enjoining men to care for their children and for the mothers of their children, the fatherhood story is society's most important contrivance for shaping male identity. For men, marriage is the precondition, the enabling context for fatherhood as a social role. Why? Because marriage fosters paternal certainty thus permitting the emergence of what anthropologists call the legitimacy principal. This is my child not another man's child. In turn paternal certainty permits and encourages paternal investment: the commitment of the father to the well being of a child. By contrast in mere nature where there are no matrimonial laws, males simply impregnate females and then move on. All responsibility for children is on the mother. Paternity is absent in the state of nature. Fatherhood is a defining characteristic of a civil society. The emergency of fatherhood as a social role for men signifies the transition from barbarism to society." [97]

That is powerful language. People who do not value the role of fathers are barbaric, uncivilized, and animalistic. Black America is in a state of emergency. I used to ask students to raise their hands if they had a father in the home; in classrooms of 30 or more students, there have been times when no one raised a hand. There have been times when children raised their hands, but later a teacher told me that they hadn't told the truth. Can you imagine a class of 30 children and not one child has his or her father at home? This is a state of emergency.

Many schools no longer have father's day luncheons or similar appreciation programs. One school attempted to recognize the men in students' lives with a program called "male significant other day," but even that vague language didn't generate the attendance that was desired.

Fatherlessness

I recently witnessed a horror story when I visited a Head Start class of three and four-year-old children. A man came into the classroom and went to one particular child to give him something and another child hollered out, "Daddy, do you have anything for me?" Both children were three years old. He was the father of both children, yet they lived in different homes. They were brothers and did not know it until the day Daddy came to class!

Research confirms that the most significant factor in the life of a child is not race or family income, but whether the father is at home. [98] I want you to meditate on that statement for a moment. As significant as race and economics are in America, they do not compare to the destructive impact of fatherlessness in America.

* Sixty-three percent of youth that commit suicide are from fatherless homes.
* Ninety percent of all homeless and runaway children are from fatherless homes.
* Eighty-five percent of all children that exhibit behavioral disorders come from fatherless homes.
* Eighty percent of rapists motivated with displaced anger come from fatherless homes.
* Seventy-one percent of all high school dropouts come from fatherless homes.
* Seventy-five percent of all adolescent patients in chemical abuse centers come from fatherless homes.
* Seventy percent of juveniles in state-operated institutions come from fatherless homes.
* Eighty-five percent of all youths sitting in prisons grew up in fatherless homes.
* Eighty-two percent of teenage girls who get pregnant come from fatherless homes.

As we review that list, it's clear that nearly all of our problems could be addressed if we had fathers who stayed home with their children. In the article "The Effects of Parental Marital Status and Family Functioning on African American Adolescent Self-esteem," Jelani Mandara reports that holding income constant and looking at the marital status and its impact on boys and girls found that boys had a higher esteem when the father was present. It had less effect on females. While girls need fathers as a benchmark for the selection of a mate and self-esteem, they are less effected than boys. The article reinforces that boys need fathers, not only as role models to emulate, but also for discipline. [100] Blankenhorn says,

> "The father is irreplaceable. He enables the son to separate from the mother. He is the gatekeeper guiding his son into the community of men. In this process the boy becomes more than a son of his mother or even a son of his parents. He becomes a son of his father. Later when the boy becomes a man he will reunite with the world of women, the world of his mother through his spouse and children. In this sense only by becoming his father's as well as his mother's son can he become a good father and husband." [101]

While we have mentioned the distinction of fatherlessness on sons and daughters it does not belittle the significant impact that fatherlessness has on all of our children. In the book *What Ever Happened to Daddy's Little Girl?* Author Jonetta Baras shares the following comment,

> "By the time I was eight years old I had already lost three fathers, Bill, John, and Noel. Each one abandoned me, each one wounded me emotionally and

psychologically. At an age when I was supposed to be carefree and brimming with happiness and laughter I frequently felt the deep sadness and abiding loneliness. Nothing seemed powerful enough to permanently soothe the agony I felt. I had no well wisdom from which I could draw to communicate any of this. A girl abandoned by the first man in her life forever entertains powerful feelings of being unworthy or incapable of receiving any man's love. Even when she receives love from another she is constantly and intensely fearful of losing it. This is the anxiety, the pain of losing one father. I had three fathers toss me aside. The cumulative effect was catastrophic. It was a potent tragedy begun even before I knew my name, one from which I was unable to escape for years." [102]

The disease of fatherlessness is clearly demonstrated in the life of Qubilah Shabazz. She was four years old when she witnessed the assassination of her father, Malcolm X, in Harlem, New York. In 1995, she was accused of initiating the attempted assassination of Minister Louis Farrakhan who she always felt was involved in the assassination of her father. Throughout her life, she was angry at her mother, Dr. Betty Shabazz, because she missed her father so much. She even became a Quaker out of defiance. That's another illustration of her defiance. She married a man who was violent toward her. Eventually they separated. Shortly afterwards she sent her son, named Malcolm after her father, to her mother. Also experiencing the disease of fatherlessness, he set the apartment on fire, and unfortunately Betty Shabazz died from her injuries.

Have you ever heard the phrase, "that's my baby's daddy?" Scripture reminds us that death and life are in the power of the tongue. That phrase has caught on in American society and it has become almost a joke. We've sunk so low that parenting does not require marriage. A person can be a baby's daddy without being a husband.

There is a state of emergency in America, especially in Black America where shacking has now become the norm. Popular talk show hosts casually mention whom they are living with and place them in the same category that other people would place their spouse. These are the kinds of images that our children and the larger society use as a benchmark to determine their own behavior.

No moral standard exists in our society today. If it feels good, then do it. It's dangerous when an unprincipled lifestyle becomes the norm and the village remains silent. Years ago in the African American village, if a man was living with a woman and they were not married, the men in the community would visit the brother and ask about his intentions. The parents of the male and female would voice their concerns.

Unfortunately, the village has grown quiet. Those who are vocal are vilified as being old fashioned and not with the times. Many brothers tell me there is no need to go to the White man's court to get a marriage license because "she knows I love her." This is hypocritical. The same brother will go to the White man's court to secure a license to drive his car, license plates to place on his car, and a license to run his business. He will pay taxes to the IRS. He will secure a license for his dog and his cat, but he will not secure a license for his woman. Shacking is done by people who want to play at marriage; they want a relationship without commitment. They are not quite sure whether they can successfully stay together and shacking allows them to live together without the financial and legal consequences.

How do you practice being a parent? How do you raise children without a commitment? How do you gain trust from children when they're not sure if you'll stick around?

There are millions of children in America who have experienced numerous men in their lives and homes. In those cases the problem is not a shortage of men (note that I did not say fathers). The problem is that the men do not stay. Baras' mother had several men in her life, three of whom Baras called father. Those men weren't just in her mother's life, they were in Baras' life, too. When her mother and a man broke up, Baras internalized the break-up as an abandonment of her. She thought the problem was with her. It is a sad commentary that adults seldom consider how shacking and other unhealthy relationships can negatively impact a child as he or she is growing up. When mothers allow men to act like rolling stones in their homes, enjoying the benefits of home life without any of the responsibility, young sons are watching and learning. It's a powerful lesson and can affect how they will interact with females in the future.

I have had the privilege of preaching hundreds of time, but never have I experienced a young boy who had accepted the call to give his life to Jesus Christ, holler out, "I need a daddy!" I observed the pastor ask his congregation "is there a man able to mentor this young boy?" A man of God came forward and wrapped his arms around the young boy. It was the most moving Father's Day service I have ever experienced. I just wonder how many more boys in church, have a deep need to be genuinely fathered?

We have got to bind the demons of shacking and parental irresponsibility, and we need to loose the spirits of accountability, responsibility, order, excellence, and fatherhood into the lives of our families.

While this book focuses on the state of emergency among African American males, let us not forget the role women play in this endeavor. Shacking requires two consenting adults. Sex outside of marriage and children born out of wedlock requires two consenting adults. A pimp can't function without a whore, just like a king can't function without a queen. It's tempting to blame one side of a problem. For example, in the biblical story, the men wanted to stone the woman found caught in the act of adultery, not her sexual partner, who was also a participant.

Let us not forget that in shacking and children being born out of wedlock, women play a tremendous role. My prayer is that more women will rise up and realize their intrinsic value. In the spirit of Proverbs 31, I pray that women will demand that men either marry them or leave. What would happen in Black America if African American women decided there would be no more sex until marriage? Like the Bible says, as we begin to call those things that are not as if they were, we can believe God for its manifestation.

The hardest question that I have ever been asked came from an African American female. She said, "I am young. I am educated. I have a career. I have a nice condo, a nice car. I'm saved, and I just want to know, is there a good man out there for me?" I appreciated the sincerity of the question because so many sisters have compromised and decided to shack with a piece of a man. They say God is more than able to do all things, but they don't quite believe God will give them the desires of their heart – a good man.

Some Christian psychologists and ministers believe that a woman's ability to believe and trust in God the Father can be compromised by the lack of a father in her life. Too many adult women never knew their fathers, or were let down by their fathers. As a result, they suspect that God the Father is just another man who might let them down as well. Their lack of faith leads them to compromise in their relationships with men.

When a sister shacks, she becomes unavailable to receive and marry the man God has chosen for her. Sadly, this is what happens when sisters compromise.

The reality of fatherlessness makes women question whether it is mathematically possible for them to ever secure a mate. I encourage you to read two of my earlier books, *The Power, Passion, and Pain of Black Love* and *Restoring the Village, Solutions for the Black Family* to explore that issue. In many of my presentations, I'll ask all the single women to please stand, and sadly, more than two-thirds stand up. There are 1.5 million African American women who are widows—one out of every ten African American women over 65 years of age. It is not as common in our society to see African American men who are widows. [103] This is a catastrophe, and this state of emergency is unacceptable.

Let's look at some of the reasons why men shack. Every research article I've read documents how beneficial marriage is for men. Married men live longer. On the other hand, single men drink more than they should, smoke more than they should, eat more fried food than is necessary, and seldom have a medical check-up. Married women monitor their husbands' health needs, and this helps them stay healthier and live longer.

Also, married men make more money than single men. Consequently, children who live in married homes are less likely to live below the poverty line. Two of the greatest contributors to fatherlessness have been the change in the economy and welfare legislation. Earlier in this chapter we documented how the changing economy (agriculture to manufacturing to technology/Information Age) has had a deleterious effect on African American men staying with their children.

The second contributing factor has been welfare legislation. Welfare literally destroyed the Black family. Welfare was like a one-two combination punch to the Black family. First the Black man was laid off from his factory job. He comes home to find a social worker at the top of the steps, telling his wife that if she lets him in, her welfare benefits will be denied. Black families had to endure this terrible assault on cohesiveness for almost four decades.

The movie, *Sounder* staring Cecily Tyson and James Earl Jones, illustrated how difficult it was for a husband and wife to stay together under draconian welfare legislation. After the government literally destroyed the African American family with welfare, welfare "reform" legislation was enacted under the Clinton administration. Welfare reform includes so-called welfare to work programs. These programs tap into stereotypes about Blacks being lazy and irresponsible. The objective of welfare to work is to send illiterate, uneducated, untrained, inexperienced African American women into the workforce to make less than a living wage without providing childcare and medical insurance. What is the benefit of working if you actually earn less than when you were on welfare? This climate helped to create the six-year-old Flint Michigan boy, who shot his classmate. His mother was working two jobs to try to make ends meet.

Fatherlessness

I'm in full support of welfare to work if we:

* improve the quality of training,
* guarantee a livable wage,
* make sure that child support and medical insurance are available.

The Family Support Act of 1996 set in place a more systematic approach to collecting child support from delinquent fathers.

The Wisconsin Supreme Court ruled July 10, 2001, that a deadbeat dad who owed $25,000 in child support to four women and nine children, could no longer father anymore children. Have we reached a state of emergency with deadbeat dads of all races owing $11 billion that the courts must make these drastic legal and moral decisions? Pastor and author Frank Thomas, challenges all potential fathers before having intercourse to have a financial resource strategy in existence. Men and women should discuss before sex the parental implications.

I am in full support of fathers being held responsible for the financial welfare of their children. However, it is shortsighted to take income from a father, but not encourage him to spend time with his children. It is amazing to me how the government will pull out all stops to guarantee that men will pay child support, but have amnesia about ensuring that mothers drop the children off at the father's house at the court scheduled day and time.

There is a difference between a deadbroke dad and a deadbeat dad. The former is someone who does not have income, but still has a desire to spend time with his child. Many agencies and mothers deny fathers the opportunity to see their child if they don't have money. This to me is mere prostitution.

A deadbeat dad may have money, but he lacks the intestinal fortitude to do what's right and spend time with his children. The government seems to be more concerned with what fathers can provide financially rather than giving them the opportunity to provide the emotional nurturing that all children need. States that allow joint custody arrangements have reduced the divorce rate and created an environment where both parents are actively involved in their children's growth and development.

Many fathers tell me they don't mind paying the money. That's not as significant as the media would have us believe. What frustrates them is when they pay money and receive nothing in return—like the opportunity to spend time with their children. Many men are guilty of giving up on pursuing their rights to parent their children.

Every father should demand that their name be placed on their child's birth certificate. They should not be intimidated by the mother of the child, nor her parents. Second, fathers should secure a co-parenting agreement with the mother. Many states have realized that it is not cost effective to send a deadbeat or deadbroke dad to jail. This act negates any possibility of the child receiving financial support. Some states have created programs like the Fathering Project, which helps men bond with their children, and improve their incomes. Their success confirms that when men bond with their children, they do not need coercion to financially support their children.

There are many organizations that fight for the rights of fathers in this female-dominated arena. I would encourage all African American fathers to contact my good friend Charles Ballard at the Institute for Responsible Fatherhood at 800-7-FATHER as well as Fathers on Rights and Custody at 502-692-3420. Many fathers have shared with me their frustration with father's legal rights agencies, especially over the Internet. I would suggest only use legal services that have been referred. I would also suggest reading *The Father's Emergency Guide* by Robert Seidenberg. Ballard told me the most effective way to gain children's rights is for the father to make amends with the mother. Black men must learn how to say "I'm sorry" if for no other reason than the children. Men can avoid thousands of dollars in legal fees, by making restitution with the mother. Black mothers cannot allow their anger, hurt, and disappointment to prevent their children from spending quality time with their father.

In the excellent book, *What it Means to Be Daddy,* author Jennifer Hamer describes the vulnerability of many African American low-income fathers. In addition, she illustrates that most fathers allow the mother to determine their involvement. If they remain intimate, then the fathers remains highly involved. If they are no longer intimate, but become friends, most fathers will remain involved, but to a slightly lesser degree. If they become antagonistic, due to a myriad of reasons, income, maturity, her parents, a new boyfriend, his demanding work schedule, then the father has very little involvement. How unfortunate that children suffer through all this "drama".

In *Restoring the Village, Solutions for the Black Family*, I refer to five types of fathers: sperm donors, no-show daddies, ice cream daddies, stepfathers, and daddy. There are a lot of sperm donors in the African American community, and all these out-of-wedlock donations have created a state of emergency. We must find ways to discourage African American men from being sperm donors. When sperm donors are in the barbershop, locker room, bowling alley, and other places, bragging about how many women they have and how many babies they've made, we need strong African American men to stand up and admonish them from a Christian, Africentric perspective. We need to point out the fallacy of their ways. The problem is that sperm donors dominate our society. We have more sperm donors in our communities than daddies. That's why they feel comfortable bragging and spouting off about their macho antics with women. Ironically, one of every six men is impotent and African American men lead the world in prostate cancer.

The second group of fathers are no shows. These fathers promise to pick the children up on Saturday afternoon, but they never show. As difficult as it may be to hold your tongue, mothers should never make derogatory comments about their ex in front of the children because the children will almost always defend the absent parent. Can you imagine what it is like for a mother to watch her child look out the living room window from early in the morning to late at night, waiting for a no-show daddy to appear? We must find a way to hold no-show daddies accountable and responsible. It will take more than conferences, books, and lectures. This is a demon and we need to call that demon what it is, bind it, then loose the spirit of responsible fatherhood. Remember, it is not by might, nor is it is by power, but it is by the Holy Spirit that we will be delivered.

Ice cream daddies do spend some time with their children, but they do not provide discipline or chores to develop a child's sense of responsibility. They take the children to Great America; they buy them all the ice cream that they want and then return them home to the mother, who then has to make the child do homework and chores, eat spinach, go to church and the other things the child dislikes.

Stepfathers are often the unsung heroes in blended families. To assume the responsibility of parenting another man's biological child is an amazing, beautiful, and honorable thing. Yet, the sperm donor gets to be called "daddy," while the stepfather, the true father in spirit and practice, is given the "step" label. Sometimes he's even called by his first name.

Stepfather is a European hierarchical term. It is amazing to me how a stepfather who pays the bills and provides nurturance can be labeled step and the sperm donor is given the honor of being called father.

Step parenting can be very difficult and stressful, and divorce is often the result. I have the utmost respect for stepfathers, and I encourage all stepfathers reading this book to not allow Satan to destroy your marriage, to hang in there and fight the good fight of faith, and to enjoy your children. If you do your job right, you'll bond with the children and they'll be leaving soon enough, and then you'll have the opportunity to spend the rest of your life with your wife.

The last group is daddies. They have stayed with their children for a minimum of 18 years. We have a state of emergency because this group is the smallest of all five. Everywhere I speak I acknowledge this group. I wish the opening segment of the news would say something positive to this group. This group needs our full support. They are quietly raising their children without any additional support from the government and they are doing a fantastic job.

State of Emergency
We _Must_ Save African American Males

I want to now talk about two fathers who have received an awful lot of media attention, Rae Carruth and Reverend Jesse Jackson, Sr. How could a sports star that earns a substantial salary decide, "I would rather kill the person I was sleeping with than pay child support for 18 years?" An article in _Sports Illustrated_ looked at numerous sport stars who had several children by several different women and, as a result, were paying large amounts of money for all the critical mistakes they made. Thank God for His mercy, but the Bible promises that God will not be mocked! You reap whatever you sow. Rae Carruth decided he was not going to pay and planned, with assistance, the murder of the woman carrying his child. She died and the boy born prematurely now suffers with cerebral palsy. This is a state of emergency.

Fatherlessness has reached the point where men will plan such a violent and immoral act. The love of money, the disinterest and lack of love for children, and the disrespect for human life caused Rae Carruth to make the decisions that he made. As Rae sits in prison, I wonder if he has any remorse. If he had it to do all over again, would paying child support have been so bad? Would spending time with his child have been so bad?

Although the media raked Jesse Jackson Sr. over the coals, he did not try to kill his child. He did not deny that he was the father of his child. He seems to have taken full financial responsibility for the child. He said he loves the child and is spending time with her.

The Jesse Jackson Sr. saga goes even deeper. When the story was released, the child was already 20 months old in addition to the nine months of pregnancy. How was this story buried for 29 months? The _New York Times, Washington_

Post, Chicago Tribune, National Enquirer, and other media outlets are very competitive. Why did they collectively decide to bury this story? White unity was more important that making money. They buried the story for 29 months and released it when it was in their best interest—during the inauguration week of George Bush. Jackson had planned massed demonstrations.

Many people—children, adults (male and female)—kept asking me the same question: can Black men be faithful? My pastor, Bill Winston at Living World Christian Center, felt that the media was trying to plant the idea that "boys will be boys." Whether it's Bill Clinton or Jesse Jackson, that's just the way men are. It's an insidious idea, and the society has begun to accept that shacking is okay, and infidelity is okay.

But the standard is not Jesse Jackson Sr., Bill Clinton, David, Samson, or Solomon. Besides Jesus Christ, there is an example of excellent manhood in the Bible that we can use as our standard. Joseph, who when propositioned by Potiphar's wife knew he couldn't talk his way out of it, negotiate his way out of it, work his way out of it, pay his way out of it, or kill his way out of it, so he fled as the Bible said. We too must flee from sexual immorality. He was accused anyway and put in jail. Well, because he was a righteous man, because he was God's man, because God's favor was on his life, he went on to become the second ranking official in Egypt.

The answer is yes, Black men can be faithful, and we must acknowledge the men who are faithful to their wives. The incident with the National Baptist Bishop Lyons, where he not only cheated on his wife, but also purchased a home for his mistress; and when the wife found out about it she attempted to burn it down. His church continued to support him along with the denomination. The government sent him to jail, not for infidelity, which is outside of its jurisdiction, but because of financial irregularities. Church folks responded by saying, "We all have sinned and fallen short of the glory of God. Let the one who has not sinned throw the first stone." While that is biblically correct, the Bible also tells us that God holds his leaders and teachers to a higher standard.

When I was younger I use to wonder why Moses was not allowed to enter the Promised Land. With all that foolishness he had to put up with (complainers who wanted to go back to Pharaoh), he hung in there and persevered. Why was he denied the opportunity of entering the Promised Land? I used to ask God that continuously. Then one day I read Numbers 20 where God told Moses to speak to the rock. Moses lost it that day and hit the rock. God told Moses that he could see the Promised Land, but he'd never be able to enter it.

God holds his leaders to a higher standard. When Eve ate the fruit, God did not initially ask Eve why she disobeyed. God went to Adam because he gave the instructions to Adam. Adam was the head of the house. God held Adam accountable. We cannot allow the demon of infidelity to become the norm, brushing it off with "we have all have sinned and fallen short of the glory of God." We must continue to raise the standard.

I appreciate the work of Project Alpha and the Urban League and their Male Responsibility Project. Too often when we talk about teen pregnancy we only deal with the females and not the males. We need to hold both males and females responsible. I commend Project Alpha for realizing that 85 percent of all teenage pregnancy programs ignore the role of males. This contributes to the disease of fatherlessness. Project Alpha is designed to teach young men their role in the family as nurturer and provider and their responsibility in creating pregnancies. If only Rae Carruth had been part of Project Alpha.

A similar program exists with the Urban League's Male Responsibility Project. They too believe that males need to be responsible; they need to be taught how to be fathers. Where in America do you learn how to be a father, especially in Black America? Trying to learn fatherhood in a barbershop, locker room, or bowling alley is very difficult. Unfortunately, that's where many boys learn their role in the family. I challenge fraternities to develop male responsibility programs. (Please don't think this comment comes from an Alpha. One of the reasons I did not pledge was so that I could be objective.)

In closing, I mentioned earlier, Charles Ballard and the great work that he's doing at the Institute for Responsible Fatherhood and Family Revitalization. In the year 2000 Congress passed the Responsible Fatherhood Act. This law is designed to help low-income fathers by providing counseling and economic development. Community and religious organizations will spearhead this effort. I'm in full support of this legislation because it recognizes that many men would like to be more actively involved with their children, but don't know how. They've never been taught how to be a father. In the next chapter, we will look at more ways to help Black fathers and offer some solutions to the conditions that are causing the state of emergency in Black America.

**TATE**

OF

**MERGENCY**

7

SOLUTIONS

There's so much work to be done to heal our community. In this book I've declared a state of emergency in the Black community and laid out the many problems facing Black men. In this chapter, I'll provide more solutions.

The times are desperate, but the good news is, through the power of Jesus Christ, we can do all things through Him because He strengthens us. As a community, we can be strong. We can pull through this crisis, as long as we humble ourselves and acknowledge that we've been wrong. We've all sinned and fallen short of the glory of God. Collectively we must admit our sins, and then we must repent. God will heal our land and deliver us, but we have to do our part first. There will be no healing without the admission of sin and the willingness to right our wrongs.

Education

In the education chapter, the solutions below were offered.

Mandatory In-service training for teachers on Black male learning styles

A fourth grade intervention team

A moratorium placed on Black males in special education

A Booker T. Washington/W.E.B. DuBois role model program

Rites of Passage program

Black male teacher assistants

Black male teachers

The Dr. King classroom

The Malcolm X classroom

Right brain classrooms

The Algebra program

The Meyerhoff scholars

Regional Morehouse Colleges

Student African American Brotherhood

Black male classroom

Black male school

I'd like to review some of these in detail.

In the WEB DuBois/Booker T. Washington Role Model Program I am recommending that every African

American male will volunteer at least one day a month at a school. Every blue collar or white collar male would be eligible for the program. Many schools only deal with DuBois' talented tenth and exclude blue collar workers. Yet, our society could collapse tomorrow without the labor of blue collar workers. In fact, truck and bus drivers, plumbers, carpenters, electricians, and other trade workers often earn more than African American males who possess liberal arts degrees. Both are important and both make valuable contributions to the community and society in general.

Every school, church, and community organization should implement a rites of passage program. There are numerous books on the market that will help you plan your own program. I would encourage you to read *Countering the Conspiracy to Destroy Black Boys,* Paul Hill's *Coming of Age,* and Lathardus Goggins' *African Centered Rights of Passage.* In Africa, men separated boys from women and through a rigorous set of exercises, taught them the elements of manhood. These areas include spirituality, history, economics, politics, community involvement, career development, family responsibility, values, and physical development.

Adolescent males of all races have a warrior spirit as they enter puberty. Many single parent mothers feel the only way to harness this energy is to keep them in the house. African American males are not more dangerous than other males, they simply do not have access to parents, educators, ministers, entrepreneurs, neighbors, professionals, and police who can teach them how to harness and properly direct this energy. Rites of passage is an excellent tool in this area.

An illustration of our failure with African American males is to observe four males ranging in ages from 12, 16,

20, and 24 talking with each other. I have observed these discussions and you can't tell who is the elder from the discussion. The older men sound like children. In rites of passage, older males give younger males direction. Something is terribly wrong when the conversation about women, clothes, cars, money, and drugs transcends age. We must remember the African proverb, "Old men are for counsel and young men are for war." The problem is that older males are not providing counsel and young males have a war against themselves.

We need additional Black male teacher assistants and teachers. African American children are 17 percent of the school population, but African American males are less than one percent of the teaching population. If he is in school at all, an African American man is usually the school custodian, security officer, or physical education teacher. He will be an administrator before a classroom teacher; and if he's a classroom teacher he is probably in junior or senior high school. There's little chance that an African American boy will experience an African American male teacher before sixth grade.

There are numerous states, cities, and universities that realize that we are in dire need of African American male teachers. Some of the better efforts are Clemson University and the Call Me Mister program, Marygrove College in Detroit and the Griots program, Wichita State University, Jackson State University, and Northern Illinois University, just to name a few organizations that are providing scholarships to African American male college students. The agreement is that after graduation, they will teach in that respective state. Marygrove College provides a certification program for African American male professionals

willing to make a career change. We need every state legis-
lature and university to provide additional funds for scholarships to encourage more African American males to pursue education as a career. If only universities provided African American males with the same number of education
scholarships that they provide for athletics.

Earlier, we talked about the Dr. King classroom that
would be patterned after his nonviolence strategies. Before there was a march in a particular city, Dr. King and his
staff would arrive a week in advance to train the participants on how to respond to racists who would abuse them
with water, dogs, etc. The same thing is needed for our
boys. Many African American boys have never been taught
how to say I'm sorry, my fault, easy, didn't mean to do it,
"my bad." These critical words could literally save their
lives, but unfortunately, they have not been taught. Many
African American males find these words difficult to say
when their peers are encouraging them to fight. The Dr.
King class would provide role-playing exercises so that boys
could practice saying "I'm sorry" and still save face.

Malcolm Jamal Warner's video, *A Second Chance,*
is an opportunity for boys to see what happens when you
make a mistake the first time, but unlike zero tolerance,
you have a second chance. This video and many others
would be used to teach boys how to resolve conflict through
nonviolence.

In addition to the Dr. King class would be a Malcolm
X class. Cultural videos such *as Scared Straight, Boys in
the Hood, Up Against the Wall* would be included. We
would also look at the life of Malcolm X in print and video.
We would also take boys on field trips to the morgue, a
drug abuse program, a public hospital Saturday at midnight,

and a prison. Many of our boys need these trips in order to turn their lives around.

African American males would teach the Black male classroom. There would be a maximum of 25 students. The adult teaching the class would have to be a teacher or coach. The pedagogy and tests would be right brain. The children would be introduced to algebra regardless of the grade. Phonics would be emphasized with left-brain thinkers. The curriculum would be Africentric using our curriculum (Self-Esteem Through Culture Leads to Academic Excellence) SETCLAE. Cooperative learning would be implemented. There would be learning centers, including written, oral, pictures, fine arts, and objects. There would be a science lab. Recess and physical education would take place daily.

The school menu would primarily be vegetarian. Chicken and fish would be baked or boiled. There would be no white products. There would be no white flour, bread, rice, salt, sugar, noodles, or cow's milk. The children would be taught the principles of the Nguzo Saba and Maat. Martial Arts would also be a part of the curriculum. There would be a computer lab and each student would have Internet access. Each student would learn to play a musical instrument and speak a foreign language. The Black male school would simply be an extension of the Black male classroom.

Everyone should visit Morehouse College to see African American men at their best. I've had the honor several times to speak at Morehouse College. Their freshmen orientation is fantastic. The challenge is that Morehouse College can only accommodate approximately 2,000 students. We need a Morehouse in every region of the country. Literally, we need a Morehouse College in every large city in America. I use Morehouse because there is no need to reinvent the wheel. The solution exists. All we have to do is replicate the great work of Morehouse. I'm encouraging the Morehouse administration, along with the larger Black community, to take this solution and see what can be done about developing additional branches of Morehouse nationwide.

A scholarship pool needs to be developed. Every African American male desirous of attending college would be eligible. The Rand Corporation reviewed a California scholarship program and reported that this program reduced crime by 21 percent and saved the state $1 billion. Another successful program provided counselors to parents whose children had been suspended. They also counseled the youth and made home visits. This program increased the number of African Americans that attended college and reduced suspensions. The program concludes that 75 percent of the students that went on to college would not have attended had it not been for scholarships. [104]

Economics

In the economic chapter, we discussed the following solutions:

Kazi

Ujamaa

The Booker T. Washington Trade program

City contracts

$1.00 theory

National conferences

Powernomics

Reparations

In the section on Nihilism we discussed Kazi, Ujamaa, the Booker T. Washington Trade program, and city contracts. What I'd like to do now is to discuss the last three. For the past two decades, a few of us have recommended that if the 40 million African Americans in this country all gave $1 (even most of the homeless have a $1), that would total $40 million. We have the numbers; all of us have a dollar. That has never been the problem. The problem is post traumatic slavery disorder. Throughout slavery we were taught not to trust each other. We were taught via Willie Lynch to look for differences, and unfortunately that evil spirit persists.

Many people have raised the question, "Who would we trust to hold that kind of money?" For many of our people, if you mention ministers, they would say no. This comment primarily comes from people who have not been born again, but it also comes from people who have observed mismanagement in the church. It also comes from the 73 percent of Christians who are non-tithers. They don't trust God so you know they don't trust a minister holding their money. But remember, we're only talking about $1.

Others say we should create a board that would include people like Oprah Winfrey, Bill Cosby, John Johnson, Magic Johnson, and Michael Jordan—people who actually possess more money than what's being raised. This money would be used to provide college scholarships for African American males and create a capital pool for aspiring entrepreneurs.

182

The other recommendation we've had on the table for years is for our largest 150 African American organizations to forgo their annual conference. We spend $16 billion annually at White-owned hotels. Those monies could be used to develop four regional hotels. We could name them the Imhotep Palace, Harriet Tubman Suite, Marcus Garvey Mansion, and the Malcolm and Betty Shabazz Villas. With that kind of money, we could purchase airplanes to transport conference participants.

Some say that the reason why this idea has not been implemented is that many organizations have signed multiple-year contracts. Like the sign at the construction site says, "We apologize for this short-term convenience for this long-term gain." Whatever the penalty, it would be minuscule compared to the $16 billion the Black community would recoup. But if we must concede to the penalty factor, we could agree to designate 2005 as the year we would implement the plan.

Another objection to this solution is that the organization needs the conference to pay for their annual budget. Organizations need to prepare themselves accordingly. If we have been good financial stewards then with proper planning we should be able to absorb one year of not receiving these funds. Another option is a portion of the monies raised could be funneled back to the organizations that can't absorb one year without their fundraiser. They could also have another function in the year. I appeal to the Black Leadership Roundtable that we are in a state of emergency and this idea needs to be implemented.

The last idea comes from my friend, Claude Anderson, in the excellent book *Powernomics*. We must control certain industries. It is not enough simply to own a store. We need to assess what things African Americans do well.

African Americans should control the hair care industry. We are the only major consumers! African Americans should control the soul food industry. African Americans should control Black music. When we say control we're not just talking the retail level. We're talking manufacturing, distribution, and retail. Claude Anderson calls that "vertical integration." This idea needs the respect and attention of African American business leaders.

Drugs

I discussed the following solutions in detail in the drug chapter.

Fight Back

Remove Mandatory Minimums

Mandatory Treatment Centers

Implement the Racial Profiling Prohibition Act

I will not elaborate. They were thoroughly discussed in that chapter.

Prisons

The following solutions were offered in the prison chapter.

Abolish Three Strikes and You're Out

Enfranchise Inmates

Solutions

Reward Prisons for Rehabilitation and a Lower Recidivism Rate

Repeal the Death Penalty

Separate Youth from Adults

Either Abolish Private Prisons or their Funding is Predicated on Rehabilitation and a lower recidivism rate.

One Church One Inmate
Every church needs to adopt an inmate and operate a prison ministry. When inmates are released from jail they need to have a church that can provide them with a "village." In the prison chapter, we mentioned increasing their release money to help them get a head start on rebuilding their lives.

Inmates are generally illiterate and lacking in technology skills. We need churches that can provide housing, counseling, literacy, and computer skills.

Fatherlessness

The following solutions were offered in the fatherhood chapter.

Project Alpha

The Urban League Male Responsibility program

The Fatherhood Initiative

Joint Custody

One Church, One Father

Fatherhood Media Campaign

I commend Project Alpha and The Urban League Male Responsibility project for realizing that teen pregnancy is not a female issue. We need more programs like those that teach males their role in the parenting process. Every church in Black America should have classes for fathers. Churches should address any male in their congregation who is not fulfilling his responsibility as a father.

We need the National Bar Association to help African American fathers secure custody and visitation rights inexpensively. My recommendation is that every African American lawyer adopts an African American father who is seeking legal assistance.

The Urban League and their Male Responsibility Project had a media campaign of excellent billboards encouraging Black men to be responsible fathers. We need a nationwide media blitz to further the effort. We need you, Tom Joyner! We can no longer allow Black men to brag about their sexual pursuits. Remember, fatherlessness has a greater influence than racism or poverty.

The last two solutions that I want to discuss in this book are role model programs and Africentric boot camps.

Some role model programs in American are exceptional. There are approximately 1,000 role model programs nationwide. The program 100 Black Men has been exemplary. My own program, Community of Men, has for the past decade consistently worked with boys to develop Christian beliefs. We tutor boys in Africentricity and entrepreneurship. We provide recreation and we give them a meal. Joseph Marshall has led the Omega Boys Club in San Francisco for the past decade.

Solutions

Reverends Eugene Rivers and Ray Hammond, co-founders of Boston's Ten Point Coalition, is an effort of more than 50 local churches to join forces with Boston's police to combat youth violence. The year 1992 was a wake-up call to all parties in Boston. During a funeral for a young murder victim, gang members chased a rival gang member into the church, where he was beaten and stabbed. People were stunned. It became imperative that police and clergy need to work together. Members of a handful of small churches took to the streets, chatting with kids and neighbors while disrupting drug and prostitution deals. They provided tent revivals for kids. They joined forces with the police and parole officers to visit the homes of troubled kids.

The result was a stunning reduction in the youth murder rate now described as the "Boston Miracle." Between 1995 and 1998, no one under 17 was killed. Overall murder rates for the city dropped from 157 in 1995 to 37 in 1998. [105] Their base of operation is the Ella J. Baker house in Boston, a reclaimed crack house located in the largely African American and Latino Dorchester neighborhood. It doubles as a church for the Azusa Christian community and a community drop-in center. It was named for the founder of a Student Nonviolent Coordinating Committee (SNCC). The work of Reverends Eugene Rivers, Ray Hammond, other clergy, and community activists in Boston is a shining example of what African American men can do when they come together and realize we are in a state of emergency.

The last organization I want to mention is Mad Dads (Men Against Destruction - Defending Against Drugs and Social Disorder). Mad Dads was founded in May 1989 by a group of concerned Omaha Nebraska parents, who were fed up with gang violence and the flow of illegal drugs in their community. From a genesis of only 18 men in Omaha, Mad Dads has grown to more than 45,000 men nationally, with 52 chapters in 14 states. Chapters include Maryland, Iowa, Ohio, Texas, Colorado, and 36 cities in Florida, Mississippi, New York, Tennessee, Illinois, California, Michigan, New Jersey, and Nebraska. If your state was not mentioned, you need to contact Mad Dads to start an organization in your state. If your state was mentioned join them if it's close or start one in your city.

Mad Dads performs weekend street patrols within troubled areas. They report crime, drug sales, and other destructive activities to the proper authorities. They paint over gang graffiti and challenge the behavior of drug dealers and gang members. They also provide positive community activities for youth, such as block parties, rallies, night parades, and car shows. They provide chaperones for community events and act as surrogate fathers to youth at non-traditional times and locations. They visit local jails and prisons to counsel and encourage. They also are involved in rites of passage programs. Their program is called Sankofa. The programs mentioned above are just a few of the programs nationwide, but we need much, much more.

The last solution I want to offer in this book is Africentric boot camps. Research has shown that Black males are in danger, primarily between the ages of 12 and 25 years of age. Nationwide, parents are looking for boarding schools for their sons. There are four African American residential schools in America. They include Pineywoods in Pineywoods, Mississippi, The Redemption Church Academy in Troy, New York, the Laurinburg Institute in North

Carolina, and the Pine Forge Academy in Pennsylvania. These schools are coed.

The government has attempted to address this problem with boot camps. The boot camp movement began in Georgia in 1983. A traditional youth facility costs $47,000 while boot camp costs $33,000. The government wanted to implement this program because they could save $14,000 per year. The program is intensive and is primarily for youth between the ages of 14 and 18 years of age. The program primarily runs from 5:00 in the morning until 9:00 at night. Youth receive six hours of education; there is no television, radio, or newspapers. The 70 percent recidivism rate unfortunately has not been good. There are approximately 70 boot camps in 30 states.[106] The major problem is that they are populated by young urban African American males, but staffed primarily by rural, inexperienced, undereducated White males.

It is my desire to take at risk African American males out of the urban area and place them in Christocentric and Africentric boot camps.

Before I describe my vision in detail, let me share with you that the Nation of Islam has acquired land in Georgia called Muhammed Farms. The Republic of New Africa has also acquired land in the South. The Shrine of the Black Madonna has acquired Beulah Land in Abbeville, South Carolina. They own 1,500 acres and ultimately want to acquire 3,500 additional acres. Former football star Mel Blount has two camps, one in Vidalia, Georgia, and the other in Washington County, Pennsylvania. In Baltimore, residents were so concerned about African American males doing so poorly, that in 1996, Robert Embry acquired land in Kenya. Forty boys attend the Baraka school in the rural section of Kenya for a minimum of two years. When Embry launched Baraka, he first looked to build a residential school somewhere in America, but the cost was prohibitive. He chose a spot beneath the foothills of Mt. Kenya, where land is cheap and his teachers, half of whom are Kenyan, are willing to work for salaries as low as $5,000 a year.

There is a challenge to the success of Baraka School. What happens when the boys return to the city? The Able Foundation steers the boys away from their neighborhood schools and places them in magnet high schools and private schools. The boys must still negotiate their lives outside school, where many of their friends have dropped out and become involved with drugs and crime. For some, this may be overwhelming, says Sister Jon Francis Schilling, who is principal of St. Francis and has watched 18 Baraka boys try to readjust to life in Baltimore. Her school is located in one of the city's most crime ridden neighborhoods, yet a remarkable 90 percent of its students attend college. Most are the first in their families to apply. Schilling agrees that Baltimore needs a boarding school, but wants it located in the city. "You can't take them away for the rest of their lives," she says. The future of Baraka is in the hands of the Able Foundation and the Baltimore Board of Education. It presently costs $14,000 to run Baraka, even with the small amount of money allocated for staff.

I believe every child deserves the right to play on grass. Many African American boys believe their major challenge is walking from home to school without being shot and propositioned by gang members and drug dealers.

I have a vision called the Gideon Village. I would encourage you to read the seventh chapter of Judges to learn more about Gideon. God does not need 32,000 to achieve victory. God can use 300 committed men to stop this state of emergency. My first recommendation is for us to provide more resources to Mel Blount. There is no need to reinvent the wheel. He has the land and an existing program. My second recommendation would be to offer the Gideon Village to the Shrine of the Black Madonna and the Republic of New Africa. They have land, but currently do not operate this type of program.

My third option is to share the Gideon Village with AME Bishop John Bryant. He has created an excellent program called Saving Our Sons. My vision is to take African American males between the ages of 12 and 25 out to the country. We would staff Gideon Village primarily with African American males who are Christocentric and Africentric. They would be taught biblical principles, Maat, and the Nguzo Saba. The Gideon Village possesses the components described earlier in the Black male classroom. The students would develop a business plan and hopefully the larger Black community could finance the plan and help in its implementation. Can you imagine these young men returning back to the city, saved and committed to restoring their communities? I can. (Please send your tax-exempt contributions to the Gideon Village, 1909 W. 95th Street, Chicago, IL 60643).

Can you imagine these young men returning back to the city, saved, committed to the race, and ready to start their business? I can.

EPILOGUE

I'd like to make a moral appeal to the one percent of the American population that owns 48 percent of the wealth, to the ten percent that owns 86 percent of the wealth, to all public officials, and to the White middle class. I was very pleased at some of the one percent ruling class that did not want to repeal the estate tax. They felt being able to keep two-thirds of their billions was adequate for the offspring. Adolph Hitler did not kill six million Jews. The apathetic German population who knew better, but were silent allowed that atrocity. I would encourage you to read the great works of Jonathan Kozol, Andrew Hacker, Tim Wise, and Jane Elliot. Oftentimes, Whites understand the need to abolish racism when presented by White scholars like the above. They can say the same things I try to express to a White audience and probably be better received.

Throughout this book, I have talked about a mean spirit in America. The country with the greatest amount of wealth also has the greatest income disparity. The term "third world" assumes that there is a first and second. I've often wondered what makes America first. Is it because we possess the largest gross national product, greatest military in the world, and the largest amount of wealth? America is also first in incarceration rates, homicide, gun ownership, suicide, divorce, drug usage, and the list continues.

When I first started writing and speaking in the early '70s, I used to believe that maybe the power brokers in this country did not know that Head Start, Chapter One, and Pell grants were more cost-effective than the war on drugs and prisons. Three decades later, I know that the power brokers are very much aware that the recidivism rate is 85 percent and we have spent $30 trillion and failed against the war on drugs. Educators are very much aware that special education has not returned a high percentage of children to the mainstream classroom at grade level. I've learned that the objective was never to balance the budget or to be cost effective. The objective was about maintaining the ruling class. Unfortunately, they used the White middle class to finance their programs.

America could learn from Japan. It is the only country with a crime rate lower than it was during World War II. It has one of the lowest crime rates in the world. In 2000, there were 32 gun murders compared to 13,673 in the United States. Thus, with only twice Japan's population, the United States has more than 400 times as many gun murders. Japan's detection of crimes is also superior to our own. Its 60 percent clearance rate, which reflects the percentage of reported crimes that are actually solved, is among the highest in the world and three times the United States clearance rate.

Japan's criminal system prefers informal processes of apology, confession, and forgiveness to formal conviction and incarceration. Only five percent of persons convicted of crime in Japan serve time compared to 30 percent of those convicted in the United States. While the average prison sentence has increased markedly in the United States since World War II, average sentences have decreased in Japan over the same time period.

The guiding notion in Japan is that the offender is not a criminal, but a person who should be made ashamed and then reintegrated into the community. The process, much of it informal, is reinforced by extensive voluntary community networks dedicated to participating in prevention and rehabilitation. In the 1970s and '80s, Japan had 540,000 local crime prevention associations, 10,725 vocational unions for crime prevention, 125,000 volunteers engaged in street work with juveniles, 8,000 big brothers and sisters for the delinquents, 320,000 volunteers in the Women's Association for Rehabilitation, 80,000 volunteer probation officers, 1,640 volunteer prison visitors, 1,500 employers willing to provide jobs for probationers and parolees, and 2,028 police school liaison counsels. [107]

What makes America different from Japan? Is it because they have a homogenous population? Is that why they show more compassion to its citizens? Is America contradicting itself in advocating a democracy and a melting pot while showing their disdain for anyone not White? Is America closer to emulating Rome, Sodom, and Gomorrah than Japan? There is more at stake in this book than the plight of African American males. The state of emergency has moved beyond African American males to the future of America.

In The Godfather, the other ruling families wanted to sell drugs. The Godfather did not. He believed that at some point drugs would reach the larger White community, but the other four families said, "Don't worry about it, we'll sell it to the darkies, they're animals." The Godfather was correct. Seventy-six percent of all drugs users are White. America is on a crash course with Sodom and Gomorrah. Columbine and the other schools were not an accident. Many White parents remain in denial about how this could happen in this "All American community" (code for predominately White). Columbine was your wake-up call. Guns are in and prayer is out. America, God will not be mocked. You will reap what you sow.

Throughout this book, I have said that we struggle not against flesh and blood, but principalities and rulers in high places. The power demon that is destroying African American males is also destroying the country. Frederick Douglass said, "Power concedes nothing without a struggle."

In Chicago, when Harold Washington became mayor he inherited a $3 billion budget. There were 50 wards in the city, 16 wards populated primarily by Whites and 34 wards populated by Blacks and Latinos. For some strange reason, the 16 White wards were controlling $2 billion of the $3 billion budget. In the spirit of fairness (Maat), Harold Washington said when I become mayor each ward will receive 1/50 of the $3 billion budget. African Americans and Latinos did not fully understand why Whites gave Harold Washington so many problems, but one reason was because they feared losing $1 billion.

In closing, I appeal one last time to the ruling class, public officials, and the White middle class to share power, eradicate racism, sexism, classism, poverty, zero tolerance, three strikes, racial profiling, and the war on Black men.

Martin Luther King took this struggle to a higher level. "The weapons of our warfare are not carnal but mighty in God for the pulling down of strongholds; it is not by power, it is not by might, but by my Spirit, saith the Lord." I believe God is trying to teach America something. "What you do unto the least of these you also do unto me." That is the only way America will avoid being another Sodom and Gommorrah or Rome.

REFERENCES

1. U.S. Statistical Abstract, 2000.
2. Final Call Newspaper, March 27, 2001, p. 4.
3. Knowland, Don. "The Los Angeles Police Scandal" www.wsws.org/articles/2000/Mar2000/lapd.
4. Wimsatt, William. No More Prisons. New York. 1999, p.10.
5. Throughout the book, these statistics will be referenced. Most of these references can be found in the U.S. Statistical Abstract, 2000.
6. Weatherspoon, Floyd. African American Males and the Law. Lanham: University Press of America, 1998, p.32.
7. Biddulph, Steve. "We can do better by Boys". The Age. December 7, 1998.
8. Ibid.
9. Kunjufu, Jawanza. Countering the Conspiracy to Destroy Black Boys Series. Chicago: African American Images, 1995 pp. 31-55.
10. Ibid. p. 34.
11. Inner City News.com. The Village Foundation. Washington D.C.
12. Ibid.
13. Kozol, Jonathan. Illiterate America. New York: Plume, 1988, pp. 1-10.
14. op. cit. Inner City News.com.
15. Ibid.
16. Ibid.
17. Ibid.
18. Freed, Jeffrey. Right Brain Children in a Left Brain World. New York: Fireside, 1997, pp. 104-122.

19. Chicago Tribune. "Grade School Creates Culture of Literacy". February 11, 2001, Section 1, pp. 14-16.
20. op. cit. Inner City News.com.
21. Moses, Robert. Radical Equations. Boston: Beacon Press, 2001, p. 165.
22. The Civil Rights Project, Harvard University www.law.harvard.edu/groups/civil rights.html. Billings, Gloria Ladson. The Dreamkeepers. San Francisco: Josey-Bass, 1994, p. 2.
23. Resolutions at annual conference of National Medical Association. Washington, D.C. August 15, 2000.
24. Principal's workshop for New Orleans' principals conducted Gulfport, Mississippi, May, 1999.
25. Skiba, Russell. The Color of Discipline. Indiana Education Policy Center. Report # SRSI June, 2000.
26. Block, Mary. No More Ritalin. New York: Kensington 1996, pp. 23-27. Winbush, Raymond. The Warrior Method. New York: Harper Collins, 2001, p. 45-46.
27. Lynn, George. Survival Strategies For Parenting Your ADD Child. California: Underwood Books, 1996, pp. 243-250.
28. op. cit. Freed. p. 230.
29. Sommers, Christina. The War Against Boys. New York: Simon & Schuster, 2000, p. 95.
30. op. cit. The Civil Rights Project.
31. op. cit. The Color of Discipline.
32. Jackson, Damiew. "Illuminating Suspension". www.idyweek.com/durham/2000-03-08/triangles.html.
33. USA Today. Nationline. February, 2001, p. 2.
34. op. cit. the Civil Rights Project and The Color of Discipline.
35. U.S. Statistical Abstract, 2000.

36. Anderson, Claude. Powernomics. Washington: Power-nomics, 2001, pp. 65, 138, 144.
37. Rose, Harold. "The Labor Market Experience of Young African American Men From Low-Income Families in Wisconsin". www.uwm.edu/Dept/ETI/pages/surveys.
38. Mauer, Marc. Race to Incarcerate. New York: the New Press, 1999, p. 162.
39. Ibid. pp. 166-167. African American Male Research Journal. The Ohio Commission on African American males. Rand Reports.
40. African American Males Research Journal Volume Five 2001.
41. USA Today. October 31, 2001 p. 11 D.
42. African American Men Project. www.co.hennepin.mn.us/opd/reports/AfricanAmericanmen project.
43. Lynch, Timothy ed. After Prohibition. Washington: Cato Institute, 2000, p. 91.
44. Schaler, Jeffrey ed. Drugs. Amherst New York: Prometheus, 1998, p 109.
45. Ibid.. p. 69.
46. op. cit. Lynch. p. 16.
47. Parenti, Christian, Lockdown America. New York: Verso, 1999, p. 239.
48. op. cit. Mauer. p. 34.
49. Rand Reports. Differing views on race. www.rand.org/publications/electronic. op. cit. Weatherspoon, p. 1.
50. op. cit. Knowland.
51. Coast Guard Seizures. www.fas.org/irp/news. op. cit. Mauer. pp. 143-145. op. cit. Weatherspoon. pp. 160-161.

52. Currie, Elliott. Crime and Punishment in America. New York: Holt, 1998, p. 75.
53. op. cit. Lynch. pp. 101-103.
54. Ibid. p. 104. Harm Reduction. www.uniedu/vanwormen/drugpolicy.html.
55. op. cit. Schaler. p. 77.
56. op. cit. Mauer. pp. 94, 116, 158-159.
57. What Works. New York Chapter of Citizens United for Rehabilitation of Errants. www.bestweb.net/~cureny. Miller, Jerome. Search and Destroy. Cambridge: University Press, 1996, p. 83.
58. "Drug Courts Heralded a Success". www.law.about.com/newsissues/law/library/weekly/aa112398html.
59. op. cit. Lynch: pp. 106-107.
60. Ibid. pp. 107-108.
61. U.S. Statistical Abstract, 2000.
62. Ibid.
63. Dyer, Joel. The Perpetual Prisoner Machine. Boulder: Westview Press, 2000, p. 1.
64. Ibid. p. 2.
65. Ibid. pp. 14-15.
66. Ibid. pp. 256-257.
67. op. cit. Mauer. p. 89.
68. op. cit. Dyer. pp. 3-4.
69. Ibid. pp. 55-57.
70. Ibid. pp. 157-158, 280-282.
71. Cole, David. No Equal Justice. New York: The New Press, 1999, pp. 146-148.
72. op. cit. Mauer. p. 19.
73. Drug War Table. _.
74. op. cit. Parenti. pp. 211-212.
75. op. cit. Dyer. pp. 11-15. op. cit. Weatherspoon. p. 229.

76. op. cit. Parenti. pp. 230-231.
77. Ibid. pp. 231-232.
78. Ibid. pp. 220-221.
79. Ibid. p. 221.
80. Ibid. pp. 221-225.
81. Ibid. p. 185.
82. U. S. Statistical Abstract, 2000
83. op. cit. Mauer. pp. 181-182.
84. Florida Introduces Chain Gangs.
    www.amnesty.org/alib/airpub/1996/AMR/25100296.html.
85. Children and the death penalty.
    www.members.xoom.com/inmate/penalty.html.
86. Death Penalty Polls. www.gallup.com/poll/releases.
87. Death Penalty. www.derechos.org/dp. op. cit. Miller.
    pp. 119-122.
88. Ibid.
89. "Push to reform death penalty growing". USA Today,
    February 20, 2001, p. 5A. op. cit. Weatherspoon. p. 182.
90. Double Justice: Race and the Death Penalty.
    www.aclu.org/library/caseagainstdeath.html.
91. op. cit. Cole. pp. 63-65.
92. op. cit. Mauer. pp. 186-187.
93. Ibid. pp. 94, 116, 158-159.
94. Ibid.
95. U.S. Statistical Abstracts, 2000. There are four million
    African American single parents. Estimates are 10 percent
    are African American males.
96. Kunjufu, Jawanza. Restoring the Village. Chicago:
    African American Images, 1996, p. 71. U.S. Statistical
    Abstracts, 2000.
97. Blankenhorn, David. Fatherlessness America. New York:
    Harper Collins, 1995, pp. 65, 181.

98. Ibid. p. 30.
99. "Changing lives, one marriage at a time". Final Call, January 2001, p. 6.
100. Mandara Jelani. "The Effects of Parental Marital Status". Journal of Family Psychology, September, 2000.
101. Op. cit. Kunjufu. Restoring the Village. p. 65.
102. Baras, Jonetta. Whatever Happened to Daddy's Little Girl. New York: One World, 2000, p. 1.
103. Kunjufu, Jawanza. Satan, I'm Taking Back My Health! Chicago: African American Images, 2000, p. 154.
104. Rand Reports. California Scholarships. www.rand.org/publications/electronic.
105. "Boston's Ten Point Coalition". www.horizonmag.com/poverty/eugene-rivers.asp. op. cit. Cole. p. 193.
106. Boot Camp. www.mcjrs/prg/txtfiles/bootjuv.txt.
107. Op. cit. Cole. pp. 197-199.